Secrets

Have

Weight

Secrets
Have
Weight

Norm Sawyer

Published By

First Page Solutions
Kelowna BC Canada

DEDICATION

This book is dedicated to my late brother, Kane Sawyer.

He left us with some amazing art to enjoy.

Kane had some funny views on life and art.

He once said about his art, "I wish I had more relatives, as they are the only ones buying my art right now."

It is an honor to be able to showcase his art through the covers of my books.

Thank you, Kane, for all you have taught me.

CONTENTS

FOREWORD

There are just some people in this world who enter your life and from that moment you are changed. Norm Sawyer, or "Sir Norm", as I know him, is one of those people for me.

Having met Norm through his personal blog, I've come to know him as someone who not only shares and teaches the Word of God but lives out a godly example in his life. He has a way of presenting life's challenges as opportunities to grow and display grace, shedding light on God's purpose in those battles for each one of us. As Norm has encouraged me with prayer and his words of wisdom throughout trying times, I have come to value him as a mentor and brother in Christ. He has challenged me to look beyond my circumstances, to trust God for the outcome and assured me that my strength will be revealed in the end.

Norm reveals his compassionate heart and concern for people in his writing and in real life, where relationships are of utmost importance. I appreciate his authenticity in a world where everyone just wants to feel good and hear what they want to hear. Norm will serve you the truth, but with a genuine humility that compels you to accept and face that truth along with whatever challenges you may be facing. Many can serve God, but Norm is gifted in his ability to reach people on their level and inspire them to grow in the Lord.

As you read Norm's words, may you also come to know him as a mentor and friend who will bless, encourage, and inspire you. May you see the Word of God come to life on the pages and see yourself within the stories. My life changed the first time I opened one of Sir Norm's blogs and began to read. In turn, may your life be beautifully transformed by the reading of this book.

Jami Rogers
Coleman, Michigan

PART ONE
EXPOSING DARKNESS

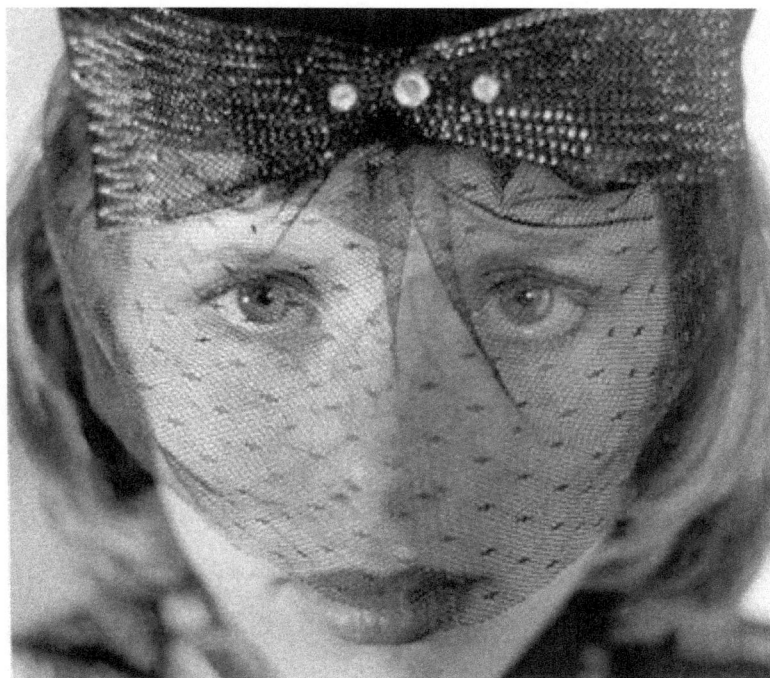

There are veils we use to cover secrets in our hearts. There are veils that some use to distract and hide the secret pain they have suffered. Through Christ, God removed the veil between man and God so we could have a true relationship. Let us do the same and heal the breach caused by the secrets of guilt and shame.

SECRETS HAVE WEIGHT

Proverbs 29:22 An angry man stirs up dissension, and a hot-tempered man abounds in transgression

Secret lives, secret thoughts, and even secret bank accounts get found out eventually. Eccl. 12:14 **For God shall bring every work into judgment, with every secret thing, whether it be good, or whether it be evil.** The weight of carrying a secret can make one sick with the dread of others finding out. The unwanted responsibility the secret contains that is affecting other people will also affect you. The secret may end up controlling your life because of the tremendous weight you find yourself under. Valerie Bertinelli said, "You're only as sick as your secrets."

I grew up with a weighty secret throughout my childhood. I saw my father beat my

14

mother until there was blood smeared all over. The smothered sounds of punches connecting with my mother's body and face were memories deep within me. I was five years old when we escaped this violent and volatile life environment. However, the memories of those ugly and cowardice events my father brutalized us with remained a secret of great weight within my soul. Prov. 29:22 **An angry man stirs up dissension, and a hot-tempered man abounds in transgression.**

In the fall of 1996 I decided to expose this heavy secret by writing the story of my young life and relationship with my father. I wrote a story called I'm Telling On You Doug. Only after I wrote it out in full living color, exposing all that was brutally done to us, did the weight finally come off my tattered life.

The key to my victory was that I gave complete forgiveness from my heart toward my father and all that he had done so that God could heal me completely. Mark 11:25 **And whenever you stand praying, if you**

15

have anything against anyone, forgive him, so that your Father in heaven will also forgive you your wrongdoing. I was miraculously healed and delivered from all the nightmarish memories. There was truly real healing that took place within my heart and life.

I have since learned to shed weighty secrets that can cause hurt. When I feel the enormity of a secret too great to carry - I drop it! Maybe you have been carrying secrets that have weighed your life down as if you were dragging or stumbling under an overloaded packsack. It is time to drop it and let the secrets out of the bag so you can have your life back and get on a God-led track that leads to peace, joy, and love. Hand over your secret hurts to the Lord so He can show you how to overcome the garbage these pustulent secrets have caused in your life.

Not all secrets are bad though. The intimate ones between my wife and I that make us smile and draw us closer to each other and God are healthy. But the ones that tear

16

families apart are to be dropped or exposed as the poisonous plagues they are. Plus, a secret should never be told that is generated out of gossip and slander. Prov. 20:19 **He who goes about as a slanderer reveals secrets; therefore do not associate with a gossip.**

Secrets that have scarred and maimed people's very souls are to be confessed, disclosed, and communicated. After this is done, forgiveness is to be given by grace to the ones who caused the pain so that God's healing freedom can rush in like a mighty wind and blow all hurts away. Psalm 91:1 **He that dwells in the secret place of the most High shall abide under the shadow of the Almighty.**

How much weight are you carrying within yourself because of secrets kept and protected by ignorance, fear, and confusion? You can be set free by giving them up and forgiving the past. This courageous act from your heart will help you take back your present and future.

THE KISS IN THE GARDEN

Proverbs 27:6 Faithful are the wounds of a friend, but deceitful are the kisses of an enemy.

Luke 22:48 **And Jesus said to him, "Judas, are you betraying the Son of Man with a kiss?"**

The act of betrayal Judas used to single out Jesus so the priests knew who to arrest is known as "the kiss in the garden". It was not the first act of betrayal Judas was responsible for. He had been stealing money from the money bag far earlier in his walk with the apostles and Jesus. John 12:6 **Judas did not say this because he cared about the poor, but because he was a thief.** As keeper of the money bag, he used to take from what was put into it. I suppose Jesus could have said,

"Judas, are you betraying me again, but this time with a kiss?"

Like Judas, most people do not become base overnight. Habitual sin usually starts slowly, with a sense of getting away with something that seemed minor at the time. There was some conviction of heart at the time, but not any longer. Now the sin doesn't even register on their conscience. What happened to these once honest people?

How did that man fall into adultery when things seemed so good at home? How did she get caught embezzling company funds when she seemed to have more than enough? How did he get so hooked on an addictive substance that he ended up sacrificing his life and family for it? When did the kiss in their garden betray their hearts?

It is interesting to note that Jesus was sweating blood for mankind just before Judas came and betrayed Him. Luke 22:44 **And being in agony, He prayed more earnestly. Then His sweat became like great drops of blood falling down to the ground.** The

Lord had remained faithful to the salvation plan of God the Father. Jesus was in the act of giving Himself for all mankind, even when He was being set up for betrayal.

This kiss from Judas would have hurt indeed. It represented the callous, hateful, and corrupt state that man's heart was in. Man needed salvation and there was no way to get it except through a willing Savior who said, "Father, not my will but yours be done."

When Jesus talks to us about secret sin in our lives, it may not feel good at the time; however, as the Proverb says, "Faithful are the wounds of a friend." Jesus is our friend. He is trying to keep us from falling into temptation that the kisses of an enemy will bring. John 15:15b **I have called you friends, for everything that I learned from my Father I have made known to you.**

Sin will betray us every time. The result of any sin may vary and the consequence may take time to reach us, but our sins will always find us out. Num. 32:23 **But if you fail to do this, you will be sinning against the**

LORD; and you may be sure that your sin will find you out. This is why the Lord asks us to confess our sins so that we get rid of them and they have no hold on us whatsoever. What if Judas had 'fessed up to taking money from the money bag? Would he have had a stronger resolve to resist the thirty pieces of silver the priests negotiated with him in secret? Matt. 26:15 **How much will you pay me to betray Jesus to you? And they gave him thirty pieces of silver.** Easy money became the kiss that betrayed Judas and he paid for it with his life.

What have you been smooching with that may cause major damage to your soul and cripple your walk in this life, just because the enemy's kisses are titillating at this time? It may feel like a wound to us because the Lord is dealing with something in our life. However, the wounds of a friend heal fast because they come with the balm of Gilead that will give us all the victory through Christ.

The kisses of an enemy may seem sensually nice at the time; however, they will carry a heartbreaking result that will leave people lonely, cold, and destitute of soul. Prov. 27:6 **Faithful are the wounds of a friend, but deceitful are the kisses of an enemy.** Jesus is our friend and He will help us through our wounded times to come out on the other side as healed, loved, and strengthened. If there is to be a kiss in the garden, then let the Lord kiss us with His mercy and kindness so that we come forth as the righteousness of God through Christ our Lord. Blessings.

HEALING FAMILY SECRETS

Proverbs 26:27 Wounds from a sincere friend are better than many kisses from an enemy.

Some of the greatest dysfunctional crashes that show up in people's lives are when a family secret is found out, or it has been unintentionally exposed. This can happen through a misspoken word, or when an innocent, or not so innocent statement is blurted out. "Oh, I thought you knew you were adopted. I thought it was common knowledge that your father had been in prison for embezzlement. Your mother died in an insane asylum, not a general hospital. Didn't your father tell you that mental illness was a problem in the family?" Many have heard worse things and it changed their lives forever.

23

Most parents tell their children to always tell the truth. The children grow up to find out that they had been lied to their whole lives because of a family secret that was covered up and deemed embarrassing or shameful. Psalm 44:21 **Shall not God search this out? for he knoweth the secrets of the heart.** At that point, how do these parents ask their children to trust them? Their argument for the family deception is often "I just wanted to protect the children's hearts from getting hurt. Can't they see that? We were trying to do the right thing." Prov. 26:27 **Wounds from a sincere friend are better than many kisses from an enemy.**

How does the family member who fostered the secret ask the other members of the family not to react in shame, mistrust, embarrassment, or deep-seated guilt? Depending on the weight and seriousness of the secret, the response can be devastating. The reaction within the heart of the one who was kept in the dark can be far more grievous than what was being covered up in the first place.

My own father found out in his early twenties that the last name he had used throughout his life was not the name on his new and real birth certificate he had applied for. In order to join the army, my father needed proper documentation. That was when he found out there had been a family secret. The anger that arose in him because of this secret caused him to hate and mistrust family members from that time on. Psalm 64:2 **Hide me from the secret plots of the wicked, from the throng of evildoers.**

I don't know all the reasons why my father became the angry, abusive, and peevish person he was. He had many abnormal problems going on in his mind and soul. He was a broken man who hit first and justified his cowardice behaviour with raging expletives. I think the family secret he stumbled upon was, in his mind, a betrayal that led him farther away from family and eventually all friendships. John Lennon said, "One thing you can't hide - is when you're crippled inside."

Joseph's brothers had a terrible family secret. They lived with a very dark deception they had all taken part in. They deceived their father, Jacob, into thinking Joseph had been killed by a wild beast. Gen. 37:31 **So they took Joseph's robe, slaughtered a male goat, and dipped the robe in its blood.** 32 **They sent the robe of many colors to their father and said, "We found this. Examine it. Is it your son's robe or not?"** In fact, the brothers had sold Joseph into slavery. This secret had gnawed at them for about twenty-seven years before it was finally exposed in full. Num. 32:23b **Be sure your sin will catch up with you.** What an emotional mess this secret caused in all the family member's lives.

I have noticed that young people today have heard everything there is when it comes to family dysfunction and outright freakiness. Many young people's classmates and contemporaries have all grown up with

26

multiple parenting arrangements and dysfunction on a daily basis. It has not made them secure people, but they have seen and heard way more than what is being hidden in some families. Letting them know the facts of what happened during their family life - whether horrific or embarrassing - can be emotionally carried when it is honestly and gently brought out into the open.

The problem arises when things are found out by accident, or someone stumbles across paperwork that tells them a different story than the one they grew up with. That stings more than the secret itself. Being babied, overparented, and mollycoddled can seem like they were seen as mentally unfit and did not have the emotional capability to handle family matters. That is what hurts and brings out hateful reactions, plus the cycle of secrecy may just become the way to handle things for the next generation. We often become what we hate.

Read the Bible and you will notice that family history is clearly exposed. There are murderers, prostitutes, adulterers, and many other sin-drenched people in Jesus' lineage. God does not hide any of it from us. Psalm 90:8 **You have set our iniquities before you, our secret sins in the light of your presence.** It is all exposed because exposed secrets have no power over you. When sin, deceptions, and secrets are known - no one has power over you or can threaten you by divulging the secret. It is a secret no more.

I am not advocating that you plaster every terrible secret on a social media platform for all to read. Keep the family mess in the house, then clean the house. Don't create more hurt than there is already. Try not to be indignant or offended by what is said. Keep the conversation respectful and react from a willingness to forgive because everyone involved needs healing.

I am suggesting that by grace we reveal the secrets that cause wounded family members to live outside of themselves. Let the healing begin in earnest. Mark 4:22 **For there is nothing hidden which will not be**

28

revealed, nor has anything been kept secret but that it should come to light. If you ask God, He will give you the courage to overcome. Heavenly Father, help us break the family cycle of secrets and the fear of them being exposed. In Jesus name!

ABSOLUTELY BORING

Proverbs 23:29 Who hath woe? who hath sorrow? who hath contentions? who hath babbling? who hath wounds without cause? who hath redness of eyes?

I cannot think of a more boring existence than that of the devil. Satan has got to be bored to tears when it comes to his role of accuser and destroyer, never to get any new revelation or thought. His mind is stuck in the knowledge of eons past, never to have a moment of the Lord's modern illumination or peace. Always the same old thing century after century, just another day to rob, kill, and destroy - oh hum, will it ever change?

Satan spends his time looking for the weak links in humanity then pounces and robs, kills, and destroys. All he ever sees is the ugliness of the human condition, then accuses them before God of the ugliness manifested daily around the world. Job 1:7 **The LORD said to Satan, "Where have you come from?" Satan answered the LORD, "From roaming throughout the earth, going back and forth on it."** Back and forth, back and forth, killing and robbing, back and forth, killing and robbing, same old same old. A pathetic brat breaking all of God's creation. Talk about a life sentence without parole.

When I hear someone complaining that life is getting boring, I often think, "Nowhere as boring as the devil's existence." We have the privilege in Christ to come to God in prayer and receive new illumination and revelation of God's greatness filling our hearts and minds with new hope. We can be comforted by the Holy Spirit in our distress. We can be filled with the joy of the Lord in a moment of time, changing our sad day into a glorious victory.

Who would want to become an ally of a boring pretender like Satan? The devil gives us poison ivy, God gives us the rose of Sharon. Beelzebub gives the world aids and cancer, God gives us restoration and healing. Psalm

31

107:20 **He sent out his word and healed them, and delivered them from their destruction.** The devil accuses our soul to the point of depression, while God delivers our body, mind, and soul through the blood of Christ giving us peace in a true relationship.

At the end of the day when the devil is trying to add up all his mischief - all he can realize is his own misery. Prov. 23:29 **Who hath woe? who hath sorrow? who hath contentions? who hath babbling? who hath wounds without cause? who hath redness of eyes?** Who has these problems? The devil does! He is simply reaping what he has been sowing for thousands of years.

James 4:7 **Submit yourselves, then, to God. Resist the devil, and he will flee from you.** Here is an exciting life. Submit your full lives unto God and destroy the works of the devil by being a blessing on this earth. Lay hands on the sick for healing. Pray for all the people God puts on your heart and see lives changed for good. If we do these things, we will not have time to be bored. We will be vigilant and aware of the enemy's tricks. 1 Pet. 5:8 **Be sober-minded and alert. Your adversary the devil prowls around like a roaring lion, seeking someone to devour.**

We can all agree that God Almighty has never been or ever will be boring. The devil, atheists, and recidivists will always be boring, but never God. John 10:10 **The thief comes only to steal and kill and destroy; I have come that they may have life, and have it to the full.** Blessings to us all.

A SERPENT'S JEALOUSY

Proverbs 26:25 When he speaks graciously, don't believe him, for there are seven detestable things in his heart.

Job 1:6 **Now there was a day when the sons of God came to present themselves before the LORD, and Satan came also among them.** I find it interesting that even Satan cannot resist the presence of God. Why does he show up to present himself before God when everything in his heart is only hate? We see Satan showing up on another occasion to accuse a man in front of God. Zech. 3:1 **Then he showed me Joshua the high priest standing before the angel of the LORD, and Satan standing at his right hand to accuse him.** Again in Job 2:1 Satan presents himself before God and in his flawed character starts bad-mouthing Job.

Why is Satan hanging around so much when he has nothing but venomous hatred for God and His created beings? I believe Satan is possessed with jealousy for the attention that God lavishes on us - his most prized human beings. This unwavering attention that God has for His people is the desire of Satan's darkened heart. He wants what we have. God's doting love and attention to everything we say and do drives Satan to envious jealousy that is so palatable it manifests in Satan's demonic stupidity.

The devil is so blinded by his own jealousy that he can't even take a hint when the Lord Himself uses His own name to rebuke him. Zech. 3:2a **And the LORD said unto Satan, The LORD rebuke thee, O Satan; even the LORD that hath chosen Jerusalem rebuke thee.** Even after this in-your-face rebuke, the devil's need to be seen and heard still drives him. This makes me wonder how magnificent God really is. It makes me think of how profound and affected we become once we have met and know God in person.

Way back when, in times past, when the devil overplayed his hand by trying to take over God the Father's realm, he sealed his future forever. Satan became an unapologetic pathological self-absorbed liar. Prov. 26:25 **When he speaks graciously, don't believe him, for there are seven detestable things in his heart.** Since then the devil has spent his entire existence trying to get back to the forefront of God's presence. I think the devil believes his own importance; otherwise, why would he be so jealous of us - the human race? I think it's because we were created in God's image, but Satan was not. Gen. 1:26a **And God said, Let us make man in our image, after our likeness.**

Pride enveloped Lucifer's identity because his name meant bearer of light. The irony of ironies after his sinful act of treason, he became the bearer of anything but light, even though he comes and presents himself as an angel of light. 2 Cor. 11:14 **And no wonder, for Satan himself masquerades as an**

angel of light. His grasp on reality was lost to the jealousy that controlled him.

He wanted to own God's kingdom and be as beautiful as the infinite beauty of God Himself. Isa. 14:12 **How art thou fallen from heaven, O Lucifer, son of the morning! how art thou cut down to the ground, which didst weaken the nations! 13 For thou hast said in thine heart, I will ascend into heaven, I will exalt my throne above the stars of God: I will sit also upon the mount of the congregation, in the sides of the north: 14 I will ascend above the heights of the clouds; I will be like the most High.**

Human jealousy will cause people to do horrific things. How much more will demonic jealousy affect an angelic being who has seen and tasted the good things of God, but now has no part in God's eternal plan except to be thrown into a dark and Godless existence. Rev. 20:10 **The devil who deceived them was thrown into the lake of fire and sulfur where the beast and the false prophet are,**

and they will be tormented day and night forever and ever.

The next time you are feeling jealous about another person's life, remember that Satan is trying to give you part of his own character so he can fight you on a level playing field. We were created in the image of God. Through Christ, we have the right and authority to cast out the devil and resist him in all that we do in the name of Jesus. A serpent's jealousy does not belong to us, so don't take it home with you. Take the blood of our Savior Jesus and be washed clean of all sin, including jealousy. Blessings to us all.

THE GREAT ART THEFT

Proverbs 25:11 Like apples of gold in settings of silver is a ruling rightly given.

We have read news articles about great works of art being stolen that were worth millions upon millions of dollars. The losses to the owners and insurance companies insuring the art can add up significantly. Art theft is usually for the purpose of resale, ransom, and sometimes for a collector's lust for a particular piece of art that ends up in a hidden private collection.

In our time in history, there is still art being returned to the rightful owners (mostly Jewish families) that are being found and recovered to this day. There was a great and organized art theft known as The Nazi Plunder. This refers to art theft and other items stolen that were strategically looted from European countries during the time of the Third Reich by agents acting on behalf of the ruling Nazi Party of Germany.

To this day the sheer volume in the number of art pieces that were stolen is vast and most likely unknown. It was looting on a national scale. We could even say it was theft of biblical proportions. 2 Kings 24:13 **And he carried out thence all the treasures of the house of the LORD, and the treasures of the king's house, and cut in pieces all the vessels of gold which Solomon king of Israel had made in the temple of the LORD, as the LORD had said.**

The enemy of our soul has been doing the same thing to Christians to this day. In fact, it is on an even larger scale than the Nazis. Satan is a thief. He spends much of his time taking away our artistic ability in praise, worship, and ministry to our God through stealth and deception. John 10:10a **The thief comes only to steal and kill and destroy.** God created us as individual artists in the faith. We were created in the image of God and part of that image is the ability to create music, song, dance, and other artful expressions to declare the wonders of our God.

God has given us the insight and creativity in sculpture and craftsmanship working with gold and silver to show the glory of God. Ex. 35:35 **He has filled them with skill to do all the work of a gem cutter; a designer; an embroiderer in blue, purple, and scarlet yarn and fine linen; and a weaver. They can do every kind of craft and design artistic designs.**

The great art theft is going on in our lives every time we compare ourselves with another person's ability. This is not a wise way to live. We were created as individuals in God. Comparing ourselves with others will only draw us off-track from whom God made us to be and the particular artistic person we are. 2 Cor. 10:12 **We do not dare to classify or compare ourselves with some who commend themselves. When they measure themselves by themselves and compare themselves with themselves, they**

41

are not wise. There is no one like you in the universe. We are all one of a kind. We are the apple of God's eye.

The devil uses procrastination, laziness, and doubt to distract us from our God-given gifts to bring forth a work of art that God would look upon and smile. Please, if I may take some imaginary licence here. God, who is our Heavenly Father, will put our artistic loving piece of work on His fridge for all the angels to see. We are individually God's great works of art and the enemy of our soul is trying to rob, kill, and destroy our abilities in God by trashing and smearing our work. The devil is a rotten adversary who is jealous of our artistic ability that is pleasing to our God.

Don't let the enemy of your soul corrupt your love and skill God has given you. Use your gifting the Lord has weaved within you to showcase the love of God toward all men. If you can paint, then paint the beauty and glory God has put in your heart. If you can sing, then sing loudly. If you can pray, then pray down the blessings of God and surround people who need Jesus with those prayers. If you can worship, then worship till the Shekinah glory permeates the souls of everyone in earshot of your praises to God.

We are God's artists and workmanship. Eph. 2:10 **For we are his workmanship, created in Christ Jesus unto good works, which God hath before ordained that we should walk in them.** Be the artist God made you to be and rise up to that calling in Jesus name.

WHAT'S THE HARM?

Proverbs 10:10 He who winks the eye causes trouble, and a babbling fool will be ruined.

The enemy of our soul and those who are out to influence us into breaking God's laws have a smarmy way of stating the question: "What's the harm?" This is said while pretending to be genuinely attentive to our needs. "Go ahead, have another drink - what's the harm? You only go around once." Hab. 2:15 **Woe to the one who supplies his neighbor with a drink! You are forcing your bottle on him, making him drunk so you can see them naked.** "Come on, try it, what can it hurt?"

Temptations will come in all forms and from all types of people in our life - even our closest friends and family members. It is up to us individually not to submit to the words that detract us from what God has put in our hearts to be and to do. We belong to God through Jesus. We were created for His purpose and not for the will of others.

Our resolve to walk with God can be influenced in the wrong way when we are not attentive to the leading of the Holy Spirit. When we are not listening to the words of life God is saying to our soul from our inner being, we can end up resisting the Holy Spirit and therefore vexing Him. Gal. 5:16 **So I say, let the Holy Spirit guide your lives. Then you won't be doing what your sinful nature craves.**

We want to be sensitive and obedient to what God leads us into because it is birthed of God. We never want to be the one tempting someone into sin so that we can have our own way. This is totally displeasing to the Lord Jesus. Luke 17:1 **One day Jesus said to his disciples, "There will always be temptations to sin, but what sorrow awaits the person who does the tempting!"**

So what's the harm you say? The harm is that causing someone to sin through manipulation or stealthy tricks that cause a person to fall after Jesus Christ has sacrificed Himself for their sins is a fool's game. God will take it personally. The Lord knows the intent of every heart, whether the intention is good or evil. Jer. 17:9 **The heart is more deceitful than all else and is desperately sick; Who can understand it?** God knows us and He knows our motivations clearly.

Keeping our lives clean through faith in Christ and walking without deceit in our hearts will help us be strong in righteousness when we are tempted. When someone says, "What's the harm?" we will be able to tell them on the spot what the harm is. There will be no fumbling of words or difficulty in explaining the hurts, harms, and casualties that will come by disobeying what God has said "No" to. Joel Osteen said, "Don't put a question mark where God has put a period." Yes, I agree wholeheartedly.

We have been saved and delivered from death through the cross of Jesus Christ. Let us keep going forward in the joy of the Lord's incredible life-giving gift. Stay blessed and stay in the righteousness of our God because that is where real life and happiness is. Psalm 32:1 **Happy are those whose sins are forgiven, whose wrongs are pardoned.**

JE SUIS FED UP

Proverbs 26:25 When he speaks fair, believe him not: for there are seven abominations in his heart.

Albert Einstein said, "Two things are infinite: the universe and human stupidity; and I'm not sure about the universe."

I am a Christian. I believe Jesus is Lord! I am not defending anyone's faith or rational beliefs. However, I am fed up with the evil rhetoric that is being passed off as a holy God-inspired murder. These destructive actions taken by organized murderers, regardless of the initials they kill under, is human stupidity personified. These so-called Muslim groups who are killing helter-skelter are not hearing from God. I also do not believe they are following any basic faith in self-improvement. They are not Muslim, Christian, or decent citizens of any kind. They are thugs who murder and enjoy killing for the sake of killing.

These misled fanatics are using the name of God as leverage for their insane vengeance and personal jealousies. These groups who misquote text are doing the same thing as a self-proclaimed vigilante who claims to be a Christian and says he was directed by God to kill a doctor who works in an abortion clinic. Neither action of murder can be biblically interpreted as being led by God. Can we protest the actions of the abortion doctors and pray that God changes their heart's desires and attitudes? Yes, absolutely, we can and should. Prov. 31:9 **Open thy mouth, judge righteously, and plead the cause of the poor and needy.**

I am not ranting or making declarations of "Someone ought to do something." I am, as many of you are feeling, simply stating that "I am fed up with religious murder and the nonsense going on in the so-called civilized world." What do we do about all these complicated events? The Lord did predict that these times would come. Matt. 24:12 **And because iniquity shall abound, the love of many shall wax cold.**

The Apostle Paul states that the world would eventually decay because of the hearts of man and their rejection of God's will within their lives. 2 Tim. 3:1 **But mark this: There will be terrible times in the last days. 2 People will be lovers of themselves, lovers of money, boastful, proud, abusive, disobedient to their parents, ungrateful, unholy, 3 without love, unforgiving, slanderous, without self-control, brutal, not lovers of the good. 4 They will betray their friends, be reckless, be puffed up with pride, and love pleasure rather than God.**

Christ also said that when we see these signs, know that His coming will be soon. What are we to do in the meantime? What does God expect of us who walk with Him on this earth? We do, after all, live on this planet with all the problems on it.

What is God looking for within our souls so that we are able to overcome the feelings and emotions of helplessness that cause uncertainty of life? Luke 18:7 **And will not God bring about justice for his chosen ones, who cry out to him day and night? Will he keep putting them off? 8 I tell you, he will see that they get justice, and quickly. However, when the Son of Man comes, will he find faith on the earth?**

According to God's word, He asks us to stay in faith. We know this because faith is what the Lord is looking for within each one of us every day and upon His return. Heb.11:6 **But without faith it is impossible to please him: for he that comes to God must believe that he is, and that he is a rewarder of them that diligently seek him.**

Someone might say that I am oversimplifying the solution to the world's problems. Not so. If we actually believed and acted upon God's word in the first place, there would not be so many problems throughout the world.

I will have to take a page out of my wife's handbook for living in a corrupt world. As she often says to me when evil events seem to be overwhelming, she gets kinder to the people she sees every day. She prays for more ability to love the way the Lord loves. She makes herself walk a closer faith walk in the Lord. She deals with her own soul and personal need to submit to the word of God. In doing that she has the compassion and ability to deal with the world's pain.

That is her answer for the world's ills. I have to say I am with her on this one. 1 Thes. 5:11 **Therefore encourage one another and build up one another, just as also you are doing.** I am fed up with the nonsense in the world, but where sin will increase grace shall much more abound. With the grace of the Lord in our lives, we will rise above the spirit of mayhem and chaos. Luke 18:8b **However, when the Son of Man comes, will he find faith on the earth?**

NATIONS IN FEAR

Proverbs 29:25 The fear of man brings a snare: but whoso puts his trust in the LORD shall be safe.

Psalm 2:1 **Why are the nations in an uproar, and their people involved in a vain plot?**

With the advent of easy accessibility to travel anywhere in this world, there has come with this ease the importation of fears, prejudices, diseases, and suspect ideologies from everywhere on earth into our backyards. North Americans live in fear of losing what was once thought to be their inherent right. What is enjoyed and called an everyday right, for a large percentage of the world these rights are an absolute privilege. Freedom and wealth in most cases are unattainable in so many third-world countries

The skittishness and unrest within the hearts and subconscious of the people seem to be the new norm. The cataclysmic and bizarre events we once read about in magazines or watched on news programs are now reported on near our front steps. What was once seen as an overseas dilemma is now lurking in our neighborhoods. Fear is gripping the nations. A color-coded threat system for the monitoring of terrorist activity is a new reality. Fear now reigns in the hearts of men, and no one knows what to do about it.

As the Proverb says, "The fear of man brings a snare." The fear of man and the evil he can do brings a snare to the hearts of men and cuts off all peace and assurance causing mistrust in all institutions that were once held as trustworthy. Luke 21:26 **People will be fainting from fear and from the expectation of what is coming on the world, for the powers of the heavens will be shaken.**

What does God say to do during these times of uncertain safety and unrest? He says to trust Him and Him alone. Prov. 3:5 **Trust in the LORD with all thine heart; and lean not unto thine own understanding. 6 In all thy ways acknowledge him, and he shall direct thy paths.** That is it. Through prayer and relationship with God, trust in the Lord and not in human ability nor their lofty promises. This is God's way to bring back the peace in one's heart.

Man is limited to the world and its laws, but God is unlimited and can help in any situation of hard times and needs. Isa. 35:4 **Say to those who have an anxious heart, "Be strong; fear not! Behold, your God will come with vengeance, with the recompense of God. He will come and save you."** The nations of the world are in torment, but the peace of God is still available to those who ask for it with thanksgiving. Col. 3:15 **And let the peace that comes from Christ rule in your hearts. For as members of one body you are called to live in peace. And always be thankful.**

Those who know their Lord are not aimless, nor helpless. They do not have to take on the fears that are pumped out twenty-four-seven on all news outlets. We have a mighty God who knows those who love Him and are believing Him for guidance during these days of uncertainty. It may look dire, but as God says, "Do not worry about what falls apart around you because He has you in the palm of His hand." Psalm 91:7 **A thousand may fall at your side, ten thousand at your right hand, but it will not come near you.** Nations may fall and the inhabitants may live in fear, but those who know their God will do great exploits and live in peace. Amen and amen!

GOOD AND EVIL

Proverbs 15:3 The eyes of the LORD are in every place, beholding the evil and the good.

The arguments and discussions for what is considered good or evil have been and will be endlessly argued throughout history, as long as people who will not bow their hearts to God are determining the outcome of what good or evil is. What do all these scriptures have in common? 1 Kings 15:26, 2 Kings 13:2, 2 Kings 21:20, plus a bunch more start the same way. They all start off with "He did evil in the eyes of the LORD." Notice the evil is in the eyes of the Lord and not what the common census of the people say evil is. The starting point for understanding what evil is should be seen from God's point of view.

Evil exists because I exist. Evil exists because you exist. Have you ever made a decision to do what was wrong, even when you knew it was wrong? Every human being on earth has made that sinful choice. The decision to sin by one's own will is a decision for evil. Evil was chosen in my life because I exist. I am capable of evil and sinful choices, even when it is self-righteousness. Rom. 3:23 **For all have sinned and fall short of the glory of God.** Free will gives us the choice to follow what is evil, or what God says righteousness is.

The ad nauseam question "Why is there so much suffering in the world?" is easily answered. Suffering in this world is a result of evil. When we read the accounts of all the kings who did evil in the eyes of the Lord, the result was always suffering - for the kings themselves and the people who were part of their kingdoms. If the king hoarded and stole from his people, the people suffered by starving and dying of diseases. If the king invaded another kingdom because of a desire for power, people were slaughtered to death with the sword. Suffering existed because the choice to do what was wrong in God's eyes was done by choice, regardless of God's warnings.

Nothing has changed to this day. People choose to sin and do what is evil and the upshot is suffering. This is one of the results of our gift of free will that God gave us. If we want suffering to stop in this world, then we need to stop choosing sin over God's righteousness. 2 Tim. 3:1 **But mark this: There will be terrible times in the last days. 2 People will be lovers of themselves, lovers of money, boastful, proud, abusive, disobedient to their parents, ungrateful, unholy, 3 without love, unforgiving, slanderous, without self-control, brutal, not lovers of the good, 4 treacherous, rash, conceited, lovers of pleasure rather than lovers of God, 5 having a form of godliness but denying its power. Have nothing to do with such people.**

We miss the point entirely when arguing over good and evil having the answers in themselves. Good and evil are of the same tree. Gen. 2:17 **But of the tree of the knowledge of good and evil, thou shalt not eat of it: for in the day that thou eat thereof thou shalt surely die.** It does not matter how much good or self-proclaimed goodness we do, it will never overtake the eternal effects that evil has caused.

We are going in circles within the limited boundaries of the same tree when trying to cure evil with good. We must eat, so to speak, from another source or another tree entirely; the tree of life, or a new position of life given to us through faith in Christ. This is what makes us the righteousness of God and gives us the power to overcome evil with righteousness. We are saved into doing good works, not by the good works in themselves. Eph. 2:10 **For we are God's masterpiece. He has created us anew in Christ Jesus, so we can do the good things he planned for us long ago.**

Overcoming evil and suffering in this world is and should be our mandate throughout this life. However, this starts when we acknowledge and discern what God says evil is. God's righteousness is a gift we cannot earn through good deeds. It is a grace-given gift from God Himself, but it must be accepted by faith in Christ. Acts 4:12 **Salvation is found in no one else, for there is no other name under heaven given to mankind by which we must be saved.** Good and evil exist, but so does God's righteousness. The only way to destroy the works and suffering caused by the evil one, is to do it with what God says works. God's gift to man is Jesus the Lord and the righteousness that comes through Christ our Savior.

Arguing over good, evil, and suffering in themselves will never end, so stop eating from that tree and take a bite out of God's tree of life. Stop and consider your creator and taste and see that He is righteously good and never evil. Psalm 34:8 **O taste and see that the LORD is good: blessed is the man that trusts in him.** May the blessings of God find

61

us and keep us in Him who first loved us.
Amen!

Notes:

PART TWO
KNOW YOUR ENEMY

When we remove our rose-colored glasses, we will see with clarity who the enemy of our soul really is. We will be able to focus our spiritual growth on living a victorious life in Christ.

TRICKS AND TRAPS

Proverbs 26:12 Do you see a man wise in his own conceit? there is more hope of a fool than of him.

I have been asked a few times why I had never fallen for any of the money scams and so-called wealth opportunities that sometimes make their way through Christian circles and institutions. My reply is simply "I did not understand the investment offered, so I did not invest in it." Another good reason is that I have a lot of friends in business of whom I can bounce these wayward ideas off of so that I can bring clarity to my mind.

Remember, the only one who gets rich quick in a get-rich-quick scheme is the one with the scheme. So it works out that my friends and acquaintances in the business community are a type of guardrail in my business life and they help me make sound decisions. Is it not the same in our church life? Shouldn't we have a community that helps protect us from harm? Shouldn't we have controls to help protect our lives as we fulfill our Christian destiny?

One of the problems that arise when a believer in Christ is not connected to a church body is susceptibility to tricks and traps set up by the enemy of our soul. Prov. 11:14 **Where no counsel is, the people fall: but in the multitude of counsellors there is safety.**

I am not saying Christians who do go to church cannot fall. On the contrary, they can utterly self-destruct; however, if they fail they have a connection and a structure that can help them get back on their spiritual feet so to speak. When we are not connected or we are out of fellowship, our resistance to deception can start to falter and our spiritual taste buds can lose the flavor of sound doctrine.

Oftentimes our resolve begins to wane and we end up existing from a vulnerable place in the heart, rather than living in victory. Christa Black Gifford says it this way: "If you are not anchored in the goodness of God, you will lower your theology to match your pain." If we are not connecting with a Bible-believing body led by a submitted leader or an ecclesiastical pastoral team, then we can find it difficult to discern what the Lord is doing in our lives. Tricks and traps are laid out like minefields on the path we are walking on. The walk that was once joy is now a nervous tightrope balancing act with feelings of insecurity thrown in.

There is a reason God said in Matt 18:20 **For where two or three are gathered together in my name, there am I in the midst of them.** We are exhorted to continue meeting together regardless of personal insult. Heb. 10:24 **And let us consider one another to provoke unto love and to good works: 25 Not forsaking the assembling of ourselves together, as the manner of some is; but exhorting one another: and so much the more, as ye see the day approaching.** How do we provoke each other to love if we cannot stand each other, or run

68

away from church every time something disagreeable happens to us?

Predators on the hunt use a method of separating a lone caribou, and often a hurt one from the herd, so that the wolf-pack can bring down their prey much easier than dealing with the larger herd. That is exactly what Satan does to Christians; especially wounded ones. He tries to separate them from spiritual leadership and fellowship with one another. The evil one will put a bug in any one's ear that will listen to him as he says things like, "Look at the way she prays. She thinks she is so righteous! This guy has been spreading rumors about you. Why are you putting up with that? The pastor thinks he is so much better than you are!"

The devil knows that when two pray, it has a compounding effect of destruction to his kingdom. He cannot afford to have us walking in the power of the word with others who are also strong in the body of Christ. These methods the enemy uses are just tricks and traps to keep us unstable and self-absorbed in our walk with Christ.

After thirty-plus years of being involved in different types of ministry, I have noticed those who walk alone because of disagreements or offences that took place in a church or assembly become bitter in their hearts. They bounce from church to church, judging them like some kind of Nielsen-Rating and not hearing the Holy Spirit's leading. They can tell you what is wrong with each church they attended, but find such difficulty expressing what is good in the particular church body.

When I bump into these hurt souls on the street, market, or airport they are all nice and smiles but never talk about what God is doing in their hearts. There seems to be a calculated avoidance of the subject. If they do talk about what God is doing, it is more often than not just a form of conceit and an excuse for leaving the church entirely. Eph. 4:14 **That we henceforth be no more children, tossed to and fro, and carried about with**

70

every wind of doctrine, by the sleight of men, and cunning craftiness, whereby they lie in wait to deceive; 15 But speaking the truth in love, may grow up into him in all things, which is the head, even Christ.

My heart is that these saints that have fallen away from the body of Christ would all come home to fellowship in Him who first loved us. If you have found yourself walking your Christian walk alone because of some trick or trap you have fallen into, reach out to the church body you were once a part of and give Christ the opportunity to heal your heart, mind, and soul.

If it is impossible to return to that church location, then please find a new one and submit your heart to allow the Holy Spirit room to heal you. Will it take some courage to humble yourself? Most likely, yes. However, the grace and healing that awaits you is yours, if you want it. More importantly, the body of Christ needs you to be a part of the whole destiny Christ has for us all. Matt. 12:20a **A** bruised reed shall he not break, and smoking flax shall he not quench.

RETURN TO SENDER

Proverbs 26:27 Whoso digs a pit shall fall therein: and he that rolls a stone, it will return upon him.

There is a knock at your door and the delivery man says, "We have your new washer and dryer you bought yesterday." The fact is you did not buy a new washer or dryer, and you never ordered one. Most likely the problem is the delivery man has the wrong address, or the shipper has the wrong customer's name on the waybill. Promptly you refuse delivery of said items and say, "Return to sender."

When the devil knocks at your soul's door and offers you sickness, disease, and mayhem - in the name of Jesus, return the curse to where it came from. Return anything the devil tried to give you. James 4:7 **Submit yourselves therefore to God. Resist the**

devil, and he will flee from you. You do not accept mail with someone else's name on it. You return it to the post office or write across the face of the envelope Return to Sender. Why then would you accept a curse from the enemy of your soul, just because it was being offered to you?

The devil is a liar and a deceiver who continually tries to get you in a position of fear, guilt, and shame. Fear, because he makes you feel like you are not doing enough and feel guilty. Shame, because you have fallen for one of his temptations and are now being accused of the very thing the devil tempted you with. The devil's tactic has not changed from the beginning. Satan delivered a well-written sales pitch to Adam and Eve and they accepted the order hook, line, and sinker. The result was fear, guilt, and shame. Gen. 3:10 **And he said, I heard thy voice in the garden, and I was afraid, because I was naked; and I hid myself.**

The good news is that we now have, through the blood of Jesus, the authority to

74

rebuke and send back anything Satan tries to give or sell us. We can, in Jesus name, shout loudly as the devil is handing out his lies, "No! Return to sender." Luke 10:19 **Behold, I give unto you power to tread on serpents and scorpions, and over all the power of the enemy: and nothing shall by any means hurt you.**

We are no longer ignorant of the devil's tricks and false promises. God has given to us through His Son Jesus the wisdom of the Holy Spirit to recognize the enemy's devices. 2 Cor. 2:11 **Lest Satan should get an advantage of us: for we are not ignorant of his devices.** We now have what Adam and Eve did not have. We have the indwelling of God Himself in our hearts guiding us into all truth, plus a written record (the bible) that exposes the workings of the kingdom of darkness. We are able to overcome the enemy with the word of God that is freely given to us all. Rom. 10:17 **So then faith comes by hearing, and hearing by the word of God.**

We now have the right to go through everything Satan has ever delivered to our door and with the blood of the Lord write across the deceptions, disease, and lies, Return to Sender. Through the prayer of faith, in Christ, you can go as far back into your generation's history and return all the rubbish Satan had given to your family as well. Eccl. 3:11a **He hath made everything beautiful in his time.** Jesus is not bound by time because the power of His blood is far-reaching. He is the same yesterday and forever. Heb. 13:8 **Jesus Christ the same yesterday, and to day, and for ever.**

Father God, I thank you that in the name of Jesus, I can return all the enemy's works that came to me through times past to this day. I rebuke the lies and deceptions I have fallen for and return them to hell, from whence they came. By faith, in Christ, I wash my heart and mind in the blood of your dear Son Jesus, my Lord. I pray this blessing over each member of my family and anyone who is in agreement with me and who wants to enter into the blessing of this prayer for their own lives. May it be done in Jesus name. Amen!

DOGGY BREATH

Proverbs 26:11 As a dog returns to his vomit, so a fool returns to his folly.

The dog's behavior is an instinct for its survivability, but fools choose their own foolishness. That is what makes the dog seem so intelligent in this proverb as the dog is being a dog. And yes, we still joyfully love them even when they are messy.

The fool, on the other hand, can get on our nerves because so many of the calamities in their lives are self-induced. We have all seen it, and in many cases, we saw the approaching destruction before they did. No matter how clearly we tried to explain what their folly was headed for, we were often mocked as meddlers.

These fools are the first to cry foul when the same old cursed result comes back to break something in their lives over and over again.

Sometimes these imbeciles even ask us why we did not warn them when we clearly did. Frustrating? Yes, and disheartening when it is family members.

Why do these repeat offenders of God's word keep falling into the same old sinful trap? Or, end up returning to their vomit per se. Prov. 23:35 **"They struck me," you will say, "but I was not hurt; they beat me, but I did not feel it. When shall I awake? I will seek another drink."**

The first reason for falling for the same old thing is that they like the sin and titillation of it. God remarks that sin is pleasurable for a season, but He makes it clear that the wages of sin is still death. Heb. 11:25 **Choosing rather to suffer affliction with the people of God, than to enjoy the pleasures of sin for a season.** They enjoy the temporary pleasures of the sin for a season, even though there are consequences and a resulting unrighteous folly.

The other reason is why would the devil change his tactics toward them if the same old thing keeps working over and over again. Bondage is bondage and becomes set in the heart of the foolish, and like a dog, returns to the sin their iniquity chooses. Eccl. 1:9 **The thing that hath been, it is that which shall be; and that which is done is that which shall be done: and there is no new thing under the sun.**

The fools think they can control the sin without affecting the laws that God set in place. They think they are smarter than gravity, so they jump and are astonished when everything crashes. We do not control God's laws; we live by them in order to control our selfishness.

We read the story of King Nebuchadnezzar. He was warned through a dramatic dream that if he did not repent of his sin and pride he would be removed from power. Daniel interpreted the vision and sets out the wisdom needed to reverse the judgment about to happen. Dan. 4:27 **Wherefore, O king, let my counsel be acceptable unto thee, and break off thy sins by righteousness, and**

80

thine iniquities by shewing mercy to the poor; if it may be a lengthening of thy tranquillity.

The king was given twelve months to line up his heart with the instruction of God. However, pride is a ruthless master. Dan. 4:30 **The king spake, and said, "Is not this great Babylon, that I have built for the house of the kingdom by the might of my power, and for the honour of my majesty?" 31 While the word was in the king's mouth, there fell a voice from heaven, saying, "O king Nebuchadnezzar, to thee it is spoken; The kingdom is departed from thee."**

God will not come down to our level of spiritual measurement as we humans have a tendency to corrupt that which is holy. Our choice to keep rejecting the word of God will have dire and ominous consequences. Dan. 4:33 **The same hour was the thing fulfilled upon Nebuchadnezzar: and he was driven from men, and did eat grass as oxen, and his body was wet with the dew of heaven,**

**till his hairs were grown like eagles'
feathers, and his nails like birds' claws.**

After seven years of acting worse than a
dog, the king is given his mind back to make a
decision. He makes the right one. Dan. 4:37
**Now I Nebuchadnezzar praise and extol
and honour the King of heaven, all whose
works are truth, and his ways judgment:
and those that walk in pride he is able to
abase.**

Isn't that what foolishness is? Obedience to
our stubborn pride. Thank God we live in the
dispensation of grace and mercy that is
flowing over us continually. Do we actually
have to go through what the king went
through to find out we are not going to win
salvation in our own way?

God has the total answer to everything in
life. He invites us to His heart through Jesus
Christ. John 14:6 **Jesus saith unto him, I am
the way, the truth, and the life: no man
comes unto the Father, but by me.** The dog
has a reason for its behavior. We need to stop

acting puppy-dumb and grow up to be mature citizens in the kingdom of God.

THE END OF THE WORLD

Proverbs 8:29 When he gave to the sea his decree, that the waters should not pass his commandment: when he appointed the foundations of the earth.

Yup, another end of the world announcement from a so-called end of the world predictor. I saw the ominous prediction on the cover of a news magazine this week. Another doomsday scenario that I and the rest of the world cannot escape, at least according to the article. It is all over for me and mankind.

I can remember the end of the world predictions my whole life, even way back in grade school in the 1950s when students were asked to get under their school desks practicing surviving a nuclear blast. I'm not sure what the teachers thought they would do if there was an explosion, because our desks were not going to protect us from anything disastrous or of major destruction. I reckon they had to be seen as doing something at that time.

What is it about these end of the world predictions that pop up on a regular basis? Yes, the word of God tells us of a time of great tribulation, but all these world events are signs pointing to that time. Matt. 24:6 **And ye shall hear of wars and rumours of wars: see that ye be not troubled: for all these things must come to pass, but the end is not yet.**

Jesus tells us not to be troubled by what we see, but to continue living in Him by faith. I am not saying we should walk around aimlessly saying, "Que sera sera," as we do have to take life seriously, but not at the cost of our peace. Phil. 4:7 **And the peace of God, which passes all understanding, shall keep your hearts and minds through Christ Jesus.**

As I thought about the end of the world prediction, I realized that the end of the world had already happened to me years ago when I accepted Christ as my Lord and Savior. I am playing with words here, but when Jesus became the Lord of my life it was the end of the world as I knew it. 2 Cor. 5:17 **Therefore if any man be in Christ, he is a new creature: old things are passed away; behold, all things are become new.**

I am no longer a citizen of this world system, nor do I live according to its humanistic beliefs. I am a citizen of the kingdom of God and His realm. Eph. 2:19 **Now therefore ye are no more strangers and foreigners, but fellow citizens with the saints, and of the household of God.**

When we became Christians and devoted our lives to God, it was the end of the world for us so to speak. We no longer served our old human desires and nature, but we became servants of the most high God.

Before Saul was on his way to Damascus and had his world-changing encounter with

Jesus the risen Lord, he was entrenched in Israel's religious system. Once it was revealed to him that Jesus was Lord, the world as he knew it ended. The radical change in Saul was so earth-shattering to him that he became the Apostle Paul and wrote most of the New Testament as we know it. It truly was the end of the world he once knew. Phil. 3:8 **More than that, I count all things to be loss in view of the surpassing value of knowing Christ Jesus my Lord, for whom I have suffered the loss of all things, and count them but rubbish so that I may gain Christ.**

What worldliness is still reigning in your heart? Do you need an end of the world experience to overcome that particulate bondage? Thinking about it in this light may not be so bad of an idea for some of us to overcome the unwanted worldliness per se.

Jesus admonished us not to worry about what the world could do to us because He had overcome the world. As far as Jesus is concerned, the end of the world and its hold

87

on us ended. John 16:33 **I have told you these things, so that in me you may have peace. In this world you will have trouble. But take heart! I have overcome the world.**

Putting God first in our hearts and lives will cause us to overcome the things that bring fear and doubt to our hearts. The kingdom of God is a place and dominion where we can reign with Christ and be in the world where we live, but not subject to its influences. The enemy of our soul uses the fears that cause insecurity and inferiority to challenge the kingdom of God and our residency within it.

Do not fear the onslaught of futuristic predictions that speak of non-stop destruction of this earth. The earth is the Lord's. If we are in Him, we will overcome the fears the end of the world predictions can cause. We do not have a spirit of fear reigning within us. 2 Tim. 1:7 **For God hath not given us the spirit of fear; but of power, and of love, and of a sound mind.** We are in Christ, the King of kings and the Lord of lords. It is He who owns us. There is no end for us who are in Christ because we will live forever with our Lord. Amen!

EFFECTIVE IMMEDIATELY

Proverbs 11:26 He that withholds corn, the people shall curse him: but blessing shall be upon the head of him that sells it.

I work in the fraud protection industry and every once in a while something changes in policy or regulations. A formal notice makes its way across my desk with a bold statement of "Effective Immediately this policy change has been made and will commence this date." From that point on we adjust our thinking and verbiage to accommodate the new rules and regulations from the companies and their underwriters. The action is swift and immediate, leaving no one in doubt as to how things will be done from now on.

What about our Christian lives? What do we do when the Holy Spirit points something out in our heart that is not what He expects of

90

us? When we find out that we have been doing or eating something that is slowly killing us, we should get this big flashing sign in our minds that proclaims, "Effective Immediately this activity will stop, or effective immediately, by grace this is what I am going to do from now on!" Col. 3:23 **And whatsoever ye do, do it heartily, as to the Lord, and not unto men.**

My wife had made a statement recently that caused me to think about her choice of words. She has noticed that the world has gone crazy and there is nothing that government, financial conglomerates, or medical institutions can do about it. These once pillars of our society who provided the corn per se for a healthy existence have become a melting pot of liars, thieves, and quacks who are hoarding what the nations need to flourish and have brought a curse on our land. (Paraphrased by me.) My wife is more polite than I am. Prov. 11:26 **He that withholds corn, the people shall curse**

him: but blessing shall be upon the head of him that sells it.

She said, "The world has come to an end, so I am going to change it by being kind, generous, loving, and living in peace. I am starting this change, first with myself. I will create a new world." There it is, saints, effective immediately I am changing things. Phil. 4:13 **I can do all things through Christ which strengthens me.**

I have to say that after I heard her declaration of purpose, I was influenced and started waxing eloquent in thought. A Shakespearean moment of "We few, we happy few, we band of brothers" came to mind. In the middle of all the madness and nonsense that is prevalent in this world, my wife came up with a wonderful God thought saying, "I will change." Is this the reverse of the parable of the tares that were sown among good seed? Matt. 13:25 **But while men slept, his enemy came and sowed tares among the wheat, and went his way.**

Should this be our covert plan to go and sow good seed among the tares in the world? Maybe that is what Jesus was trying to get across to us when He ministered His sermon on the Mount. Matt. 5:44 **But I say unto you, "Love your enemies, bless them that curse you, do good to them that hate you, and pray for them which despitefully use you, and persecute you."** Jesus was saying, "Hey! Get out there and change the world, but first start with your own hearts. Get out there and sow some good seed among the tares and be a world changer."

The procrastination that has become commonplace in our society as in I will get out of debt one day; I will start a garden one day; I will start a healthier lifestyle one day; I will start praying more often one day; I will connect with my family more often one day, and so on and so on is draining us of life. Perhaps place a notice across our hearts that says, "Effective immediately, I am going to be who God made me to be." 2 Cor. 6:2 **For God says, "At just the right time, I heard** you. **On the day of salvation, I helped you."** Indeed, the "right time" is now. Today is the day of salvation.

Today is the day to start changing our world. Deut. 30:19 **Today I have given you the choice between life and death, between blessings and curses. Now I call on heaven and earth to witness the choice you make. Oh, that you would choose life, so that you and your descendants might live!** God is cheering us on to make some life choices that can affect everyone around us. We just have to respond with "Effective immediately, I choose life, Lord!"

HEAD GAMES

Proverbs 29:11 A fool utters all his mind: but a wise man keepeth it in till afterwards.

Louis Pasteur said, "Chance favors the prepared mind."

The head games being played out for our attention, money, and time is chasing us down at accelerated speeds. The thousands of daily ads and noises rushing toward us on a continual basis is causing a social weariness and numbness within the hearts of many. Tired minds have become the default setting in people of all social standings around the world.

The inability to focus on the task at hand is causing a desire within these people to look for an escape to anywhere but here. Psalm 55:6 **I said, "Oh, that I had wings like a dove! I would fly away and be at rest."**

How do we get control of our minds so we are at peace within our own lives and with each other? Is it possible to keep the worldly head games from playing out their agendas within us? How do we let our minds be in Christ so we are at peace in our souls?

The answer may be too simple, but nonetheless, it is a good answer. Phil. 2:5 **Let this mind be in you, which was also in Christ Jesus.** The more we know Jesus, the more we know who we are in Christ. The more we know who we are in Christ, the more we will be at peace in our minds. The Lord says we who are in Christ are the light of the world. If God says we are His light in this world, then let us turn on that light to its full brilliance. If Jesus is our Lord, then let us grow up in His Lordship so we may be the light and salt of the earth and mature into who God wants us to be. Eph. 4:14 **Then we will no longer be infants, tossed about by the waves and carried around by every wind of teaching and by the clever**

cunning of men in their deceitful scheming.

When our minds are set on God, we will recognize the head games when they come our way asking us to play. We will be able to give the game a confident "No, I don't want to play." The Lord has given us a sound mind, or the ability to be disciplined in mind through the indwelling of the Holy Spirit within our soul. Heb. 4:12 **For the word of God is living and active, sharper than any two-edged sword, piercing to the division of soul and of spirit, of joints and of marrow, and discerning the thoughts and intentions of the heart.**

In doing this, God is able to help us change our position of existence to be what God says we are. We do not have to be overwhelmed by all the head games that often traumatize individuals into a place of pitiful existence. If God says we have a sound mind, then let us step forward by faith and exercise this truth. 2 Tim. 1:7 **For God hath not given us the**

spirit of fear; but of power, and of love, and of a sound mind.

We can focus on what God has put in our minds; however, we have to keep bringing the plan of God to the forefront of our minds. It is a daily act of faith and declaration on our part because the onslaught of the enemy is continually coming at us with his daily demonic rhetoric. Therefore, we must daily renew our minds in the word of God. Rom. 12:2 **Do not be conformed to this world, but be transformed by the renewing of your mind. Then you will be able to discern what is the good, pleasing, and perfect will of God.**

Someone might ask if this barrage of daily attacks on the Christian life and mind will ever let up? No! As long as we are living on this side of the grave, it will never let up. However, we who are practicing the life and presence of the Lord will keep overcoming because the Lord of Glory will keep leading us into His victory.

The blessings of God favors the prepared mind in Christ. Even though we have eternal life, we have to remember that we live in a day to day relationship with the Lord. Our strength is renewed day by day through the victory Jesus acquired for us with His perfect and holy sacrifice. Isa. 26:3 **You will keep in perfect peace those whose minds are steadfast, because they trust in you.** Peace of mind be with us all, in Jesus name.

DEBTORS' PRISON

Proverbs 22:7 The rich rule over the poor, and the borrower is slave to the lender.

The old hymn describes it clearly: "He paid a debt He did not owe, I owed a debt I could not pay, I needed someone to wash my sins away."

We were all headed for eternal debtors' prison until Jesus paid our debt in full with His blood sacrifice. Debtors' prison as described by Wikipedia was a place where destitute people who were unable to pay a court-ordered judgment would be incarcerated (usually similar in form to locked workhouses) until they had worked off their debt, via labor or secured outside funds to pay the balance. The product of their labor went towards both the costs of their incarceration and their accrued debt.

Jesus spent so much of His ministry time trying to equip us from falling into sinful debt. The wages of sin is death. The cost of death is eternal debtors' prison. The Lord Jesus came to deliver us from this eternal judgment. 2 Cor. 5:21 **For God made Christ, who never sinned, to be the offering for our sin, so that we could be made right with God through Christ.** What an amazing feat our Lord and Savior pulled off for any and every person who would receive His gift of sacrificial love by faith. John 3:16 **For God so loved the world that He gave His only begotten Son, that whoever believes in Him should not perish but have everlasting life.**

When we finally find out who we are in Christ, we will also work toward helping people stay out of debtors' prison so to speak. We have been given the ministry of reconciliation. 2 Cor. 5:18 **Everything is from God, who has reconciled us to himself through Christ and has given us the ministry of reconciliation.** This was done so that we could help those break out of debtors' prison and become God's children in His kingdom. Being in debt to anyone but Christ is a mug's game that will leave you hopeless and eternally destitute. As the Proverb says, you will eventually mount up debt to the point of becoming a slave to it.

If this principle is true in everyday life, then how much more will it be a fact in your spiritual life? If you have creditors knocking on your door demanding payment for stuff purchased on credit but now you are penniless - the debt does not go away. It surely will be paid somehow and at some time. However, your life will not be your own as it will belong to the creditors. Prov. 22:7 **The rich rule over the poor, and the borrower is slave to the lender.**

This is what happened to Adam and Eve when they sinned through their disobedience toward God. They became slaves to sin and found out in a short time that the wages of sin is death. Gen. 3:19 **By the sweat of your brow will you have food to eat until you**

102

return to the ground from which you were made. For you were made from dust, and to dust you will return. They became separated from an intimate relationship with God because of the sin they had committed. In order to escape the debtors' prison, man was now in need of grace. There was absolutely nothing man could do to pay for the eternal tormenting result that sin had caused. Rom. 7:24 **Oh, what a miserable person I am! Who will free me from this life that is dominated by sin and death?**

The good news is that Jesus paid our debt in full through the work of the cross and blood sacrifice He gave out of His love for us. We were bailed out of debtors' prison. All we have to do is accept the Lord's gift by faith. Now that we are out of death's debt, we can bring life to those who are seeking deliverance from the slavery many have found themselves to be in. Prov. 3:27 **Do not withhold good from those to whom it is due, when it is in your power to do it.**

Let us commit to staying away from sin because as someone once said, "Sinning is empowering Satan to speak on your behalf." Well, saints, the devil will not speak for me as I have been paid for in full by the blood of the Lord who keeps me out of the jailer's hands. Blessings to you all.

THE SINS OF ANGELS

Proverbs 16:18 Pride comes before destruction, and an arrogant spirit before a fall.

Ezekiel 28:17a **Your heart was filled with pride because of all your beauty. Your wisdom was corrupted by your love of splendor.** Lucifer and the angels who fell in sin were filled with pride and vanity of their magnificence. It is no wonder that the temptation offered to Adam and Eve was birthed in the sin of pride. Gen. 3:5 **In fact, God knows that when you eat it your eyes will be opened and you will be like God, knowing good and evil.** Imagine being tempted to be like God. The insidiousness of the sin of pride cannot be overstated. Satan tempted Eve from the depths of the envious pride that was now permanently part of Satan's character.

105

We could say that this prideful vanity found in the hearts of the fallen angels is the zeitgeist of our time. The narcissistic behavior and puffed up self-image that many people have of themselves has found its way into the very persona of our generation. "My opinion is my god, and you cannot dethrone me with your opinion" is said with force from all manners of media platforms and acted out in crass exhibitionism. Hubris and arrogance have taken over their minds and they have lost their ability to blush. Vulgar expletives have become their spoken words. Prov. 14:3a **A fool's mouth lashes out with pride.**

The sins of angels are powerful temptations to overcome because these angelic beings were, in fact, so beautiful. If supernatural beings like angels could not control the pull of these sins, then what makes humans think they can resist the temptation of pride in their own strength? All sin is rooted in pride, envy, and vanity. We need a savior who defeated sin in all its ugliness. Plus, He has the ability to bring us into a position of righteousness -

because of the power of Jesus' blood that was shed for us. We need Christ guiding our thoughts and intentions of our heart to overcome the slithering wickedness that results from acting out in pride.

Why is pride so destructive to the human soul? Because it causes mankind to stop seeking, longing, and praying to God. Psalm 10:4 **The wicked, through the pride of his countenance, will not seek after God: God is not in all his thoughts.** This is what happened to Lucifer when envious pride filled his heart. He felt he could take God out of the picture so to speak. He thought he was greater than God. Prideful vanity distorts the image within one's heart and mind.

Lucifer thought he could reign over God, rather than serve Him. Isa. 14:13 **For thou hast said in thine heart, I will ascend into heaven, I will exalt my throne above the stars of God: I will sit also upon the mount of the congregation, in the sides of the north: 14 I will ascend above the heights of the clouds; I will be like the**

most High. Lucifer imagined he would rule, but the exact opposite took place. He was cast out of heaven at the speed of lightning. Luke 10:18 **He said to them, "I watched Satan fall from heaven like lightning."** The sin of pride sealed Satan's fate forever. Isa. 14:15 **Yet thou shalt be brought down to hell, to the sides of the pit.**

If we want to be exalted in life, God says to humble ourselves under the mighty hand of God. 1 Pet. 5:6 **Humble yourselves therefore under the mighty hand of God, that he may exalt you in due time.** It is so incredible that God humbled Himself and came to earth as a man. If God uses humility to reach us in love, then we too can be humble in our hearts when expressing love and submitting to our Heavenly Father.

There is no need for pride, envy, or vanity when we are in communion with our God. These sins of angels only show up in our lives when we forget to walk in forthrightness with our Lord. Don't let Satan give you part of his character. Happy is the man who walks with

108

no sins weighing him down. Psalm 32:1 **How joyful is the one whose transgression is forgiven, whose sin is covered!** Do you want victory over pride? Then give all unrighteous pride back to the enemy from whence it came. May real peace fill your lives. Amen!

THERE'S NO END

Proverbs 11:18 A wicked person earns deceptive wages, but the one who sows righteousness reaps a sure reward.

I was driving behind a car that had a bumper sticker that said *There's No End* written with white letters on black background in a Gothic-dripping font. I thought, "That's an ominous and hopeless looking message." Then I thought, "This message is true." There is no end to this world system unless we do something about it. There is no end to an uninspired redundant life. Life will feel like dripping hopelessness unless we do something about it.

Unless we change our story, there will be no end to our chasing of the wind so to speak. Countless millions of people get up every day doing the same old thing with drudgery in their hearts and a foreboding sense of what is

110

the point to this endless repetitiveness of just existing? Eccl. 2:18 **But as I looked at everything I had worked so hard to accomplish, it was all so meaningless— like chasing the wind. There was nothing really worthwhile anywhere.**

There is no end to this earthbound existence until we change the story we are living in and start thinking heaven bound. Until we realize God's goodness toward us and begin to say and repeat what God says about our divine creation and purpose for being here, we will not find our God-given and designed destiny. Until we do something that is God-centered and inspired, our story will not change. Until we enter into what God has prepared for those who love Him, there will be no end to the dull, insipid, nerve numbing existence that so many trudge along in.

As Jesus said, "I have come that they may have life, and have it to the full." When we have a God-centered life within us, we will stop and consider God's love toward us. Psalm 8:3 **When I consider your heavens,** the work of your fingers, the moon and the stars, which you have set in place, 4 what is mankind that you are mindful of them, human beings that you care for them?**

There's no end in sight if we do not have a vision for the Lord's life within us. When we enter His presence, we begin to find our way. Psalm 73:17 **Only when I came into God's holy place did I finally understand what would happen to them.** With God's leading, we will find the Lord's reason and purpose for our lives. We will become overjoyed with the fact there's no end because our eternity is with the mighty God who will forever be expanding our existence to unimaginable and euphoric heights. Rom. 8:18 **For I consider that the sufferings of this present time are not worth comparing with the glory that is going to be revealed to us.**

How true this Proverb. **A wicked person earns deceptive wages, but the one who sows righteousness reaps a sure reward.** Keep working without the Lord in the world system and there's no end to its life-sapping existence. Enter the righteousness of God through Christ and there's no end to the joy, blessing, fulfillment, and love God sows within our hearts to discover and live by. Thank you, Lord, in you there's no end to your love for us. Jer. 31:3 **The LORD appeared to us in the past, saying: "I have loved you with an everlasting love; I have drawn you with unfailing kindness."** Yes, Lord, in you there's no end to your love and kindness.

AN EMOTIONAL LIE

Proverbs 17:4 An evildoer listens to wicked lips, and a liar gives ear to a mischievous tongue.

Adam and Eve had been living a protected and blessed life in the garden of Eden. Eve was used to straight talk with Adam and God. "What is that Adam?" "That is an Elephant." "What is that God?" "That is the tree of life." "And that one?" "That is the tree of the knowledge of good and evil. Do not ever eat from it or you will die." Gen. 2:16 **And the LORD God commanded the man, saying, of every tree of the garden you may freely eat: 17 but of the tree of the knowledge of good and evil you shall not eat, for in the day that you eat of it you shall surely die.**

I believe the everyday communication Eve had with the Lord and Adam was honest and to the point. Eve was emotionally safe because her conversations had no ambiguity, cynicism, or crassness in it. The communication Eve experienced was clean and pure.

Then the devil came along, lied to Eve, and tricked her into distrusting the integrity of God. The devil said to Eve, "Did God really say you must not eat the fruit from any of the trees in the garden?" When defending what someone said, it is easy to become emotionally responsive as Eve did. It was an emotional lie Eve fell for and resulted in her wanting something more than God could or would give her at the time. Gen. 3:6 **And when the woman saw that the tree was good for food, and that it was pleasant to the eyes, and a tree to be desired to make one wise, she took of the fruit thereof, and did eat, and gave also unto her husband with her; and he did eat.**

Judas also fell for an emotional lie while walking with Jesus for three years. Judas betrayed Jesus at the last supper. John 13:27a **After Judas took the piece of bread, Satan**

115

entered into him. There was a belief that a Messiah was going to deliver the chosen people from their oppressors. The Lord was trying to save mankind from eternal oppression and death, but Judas was trying to provoke Jesus into saving Israel from Roman oppression. Judas believed the emotional argument the religious leaders put forth. Prov. 17:4 **An evildoer listens to wicked lips, and a liar gives ear to a mischievous tongue.** Judas' emotions were right off the chart. When he realized what he had done, he ended up committing suicide and paid dearly for his sin.

It does not seem to matter how long we have walked with the Lord, or have overcome past temptations. There are always new temptations coming along to test us one more time. The sin we take part in that seemed so innocent and even harmless at the time now creeps up our spine with squeezing reptilian thoughts of "What have I done?"

That is always the result of falling into temptation, because the emotional lies are

116

always the most disappointing and crushing to our soul. It is so personal. The sin at the time was so titillating and looked to be an ultimate privilege in life, but the results are never satisfying or fulfilling. True enough, it was seductive to look at and desire as Eve noted, but not satisfying as we all found out.

These sinful ideas or desires shout "It will all be good and fun. You will never have a better chance at happiness." In the end, however, it always leaves us feeling like we were let down so hard our inner man hurts and feels uncomfortably anxious. Rom. 7:11 **For sin, seizing the opportunity afforded by the commandment, deceived me, and through the commandment put me to death.**

The seemingly harmless sin that looked good a few minutes ago now has a stench of utter disappointment about it. Now we are not sure what to do with it. We realize what an emotional lie it was that we fell for because our self-satisfying gratification had not been met as promised. Now our emotions are judging our mind and heart with no mercy.

Rom. 7:24 **O wretched man that I am! who shall deliver me from the body of this death?**

Thank God the blood and sacrifice of Jesus Christ will meet our every need. That includes the emotional needs as well. The salvation of God has cleansed us from all sins of the body, mind, and soul. We can bring our emotions to the Lord and have them tenderly touched, healed, and sorted so that we can get up in strength to fight the good fight of faith in Jesus name. Rom. 8:37 **No, in all these things we are more than conquerors through Him who loved us.** Thank you, Lord, for keeping us emotionally sound in Christ. Amen.

Notes:

.

PART THREE
THE HUMAN CONDITION

The human condition is in constant need of God's help and grace to enable us to remove our masks. We often think we have it all together, but soon find out we fall short of perfection. We truly need a Saviour who is perfect to give us His love and ability to be who we were created to be.

EVERYONE'S A CRITIC

Proverbs 29:1 If you get more stubborn every time you are corrected, one day you will be crushed and never recover.

Norman Vincent Peal said, "The trouble with most of us is that we would rather be ruined by praise than saved by criticism."

False praise can get us into trouble and can trip us up into believing our own self-made doctrines brought forth from the gospel of self. Gal. 6:8a **For he that sows to his flesh shall of the flesh reap corruption.** Submitting and listening through discernment, the wisdom of the Holy Spirit will guard and keep us from falling into the trap of false and unrealistic grandeur caused by the hype of the crowd. Gal. 6:8b **But he that sows to the Spirit shall of the Spirit reap life everlasting.**

122

Jesus understood what motivated man. The human condition judges from a platform of trends and nuances of the majority, even when the majority is wrong. John 2:23 **In Jerusalem during Passover many people put their faith in Jesus, because they saw him work miracles.** 24 **But Jesus knew what was in their hearts, and he would not let them have power over him.**

The crowd is with you one moment, then with a Twitter storm of slander will criticize you the next. The standard the crowd uses for non-constructive criticism of others is fear-based and driven by insecurity of their own self-worth. It is hard to accept others when you cannot accept yourself. Sin consciousness will cause this behavior in people.

Fickleness and populous opinions will make critics out of everyone. We actually have the audacity to sit back and judge, criticize, and belittle God for what goes wrong in the world, but not take the time to thank Him when anything goes right. Everyone's a critic, but not everyone can build with the critical truth of the Spirit of God. 1 Cor. 2:14 **Now the natural man doesn't receive the things of God's Spirit, for they are foolishness to him, and he can't know them, because they are spiritually discerned.**

When God corrects, convicts, or is critical of our behavior toward Him or someone else, He directs us through love and helps us overcome that area of our lives needing work and change. Isa. 30:2 **Whether you turn to the right or to the left, your ears will hear a voice behind you, saying, "This is the way; walk in it."**

God's direction will be led by the truth of His word. His will for us is victory over the stubbornness of our flesh so that we eventually come under His authority and will through Jesus Christ. God wants us to be healed in life, not crushed because of disobedience. Prov. 29:1 **If you get more stubborn every time you are corrected, one day you will be crushed and never recover.**

If we are going to be critics in life, then let

the criticism be on our own behavior so that we can line up with the will and call of God. As is often said, "There are three fingers pointing back at ourselves when we point at others."

Perhaps the three points should become three questions we ask ourselves before we speak out with some ungodly criticism. Is what I am about to do pleasing to the Lord? Am I going to inspire faith with what I am about to say? Is what I am about to act out going to be a blessing? Maybe you have your own three questions to help you become what God wants you to be. Ask them and respond positively in Jesus name. Amen!

ME, MYSELF, AND I

Proverbs 3:31 Do not envy a man of violence and do not choose any of his ways.

Why are other people's prejudices strange to our thinking and ours seem right and should be accepted? There are those who are quick to point out that all of our woes today are because of the me, myself, and I generation. I do not think this is the current problem. Every generation in history has had to deal with those who are selfish and solipsistic. There is nothing new here in our outward prejudices of another's actions. We are very skilled at pointing out the reasons for all the problems others cause. We never seem to point at ourselves for the cause of things going wrong.

Me, myself, and I have been the reason for submitting to temptation and compromise from the first sin in the garden of Eden. Gen. 3:6 **The woman saw that the tree was good for food and delightful to look at, and that it was desirable for obtaining wisdom. So she took some of its fruit and ate it; she also gave some to her husband, who was with her, and he ate it.** Like Adam and Eve, I make the choice to sin, even though I may have been deceived. I have to take responsibility for myself and for the actions I choose in life.

Me, myself, and I have to choose to stay away from iniquity. Psalm 18:23 **I was blameless toward Him and kept myself from my iniquity.** I make the choice to choose or not choose what Satan offers me. Prov. 3:31 **Don't envy a violent man or choose any of his ways.** I choose to give all of myself to the Lord Jesus and I make this choice because of the love God has shown me. Therefore, I enter a real relationship with God the Father through faith in Christ. I have the right to choose God, or choose not to let Him into my life. No excuses work here, as it is me, myself, and I making the choice to love or not to.

What shall we say or do then? As long as we sit on the throne of our own heart, our choices will be selfish and self-serving. The moment we ask Christ onto the throne of our heart and allow Him the reigning voice, we will become who God intended us to be when He created us. Our raison d'etre for being created will far extend our short and insipid views on life when Jesus reigns. We have been born with eternity in our hearts and that eternity has a God purpose. Eccl. 3:11 **He has made everything appropriate in its time. He has also put eternity in their hearts, but no one can discover the work God has done from beginning to end.**

When God thought of us individually and we became a living being through birth, His vision for our lives was eternally divine and set. God could see us in eternity's future fulfilling the majestic plans of God. No matter how big we think we can vision life and purpose, it truly pales in comparison to the vision God has for each and every one of us. Psalm 139:6 **This wondrous knowledge is beyond me. It is lofty; I am unable to reach it.**

When me, myself, and I get out of God's way and I allow the Lord His rightful place in my heart, I will no longer worry about choosing the ways of a violent and oppressive man. My prejudices will not be self-serving, but guided by the spirit of the living God. The Holy Spirit will teach me what is the will of God for myself and my fellow man. John 16:13a **But when he, the Spirit of truth, comes, he will guide you into all the truth.** May we all get out of God's way so He can work His eternal miracle in all our lives. Amen!

" I "

Proverbs 20:9 Who can say, I have made my heart clean, I am pure from my sin?

I want. I need. I will. I must. I can't. I won't be much help to anyone if all I can think of is me, myself, and I. I am my favorite subject. Tell me more about myself. Why am I always worried about me? Why am I always in the way? In the early 1980s, I read a book by Earl Jabay called *Kingdom Of Self*. One of the interesting factoids he brought out in his book is from the moment we are born, we start crying and want to satisfy ourselves and ourselves only.

It takes training and resolution of the heart to learn how to share and be willing to give of ourselves from our own personal kingdoms. From Paul Tripp's book *War of Words* he writes, "If I sat with you and I listened to a recording of the last month of your words, whose kingdom, what kingdom, would I conclude those words are spoken to serve? Would it be the kingdom of self with its self-focused demandingness, expectancy, and entitlement?"

Being honest with myself I would have to say that the kingdom of me, myself, and I would have been mentioned often over the last month. It is most likely that some of our daily rhetoric on building a personal kingdom would sound similar to Satan's pathetic speech. Isa. 14:12 **How art thou fallen from heaven, O Lucifer, son of the morning! how art thou cut down to the ground, which didst weaken the nations! 13 For thou hast said in thine heart, I will ascend into heaven, I will exalt my throne above the stars of God: I will sit also upon the mount of the congregation, in the sides of the north: 14 I will ascend above the heights of the clouds; I will be like the most High.**

Oh, maybe our fists were not pointed at heaven and our vocabulary was not as repugnant as Lucifer's, but if we are honest with our hearts there are some similar declarations of personal entitled demands. Our tones and vocabulary would have been disguised with religiosity and politeness and our words may have sounded like this: "I was such a blessing to so and so. I went out of my way for that brother in the Lord and I was not thanked whatsoever. I have been serving in this church for years and never have I been recognized for all the stuff I do. After all, I did bring toothpicks for everyone else at the church picnic. Don't you know, Lord, that I am he who worships thee?"

Prov. 20:9 **Who can say, I have made my heart clean, I am pure from my sin?** No one can say, "Under my terms, I have made myself right and acceptable to God." It is all God. It is all His grace that gives us life in Him. It is Christ's blood only that makes us righteous in the eyes of God. God's terms are clear and generous toward us all. His terms and love are grace. Eph. 2:8 **For by grace are ye saved through faith; and that not of**

yourselves: it is the gift of God: 9 **Not of works, lest any man should boast.**

The kingdom of self will be at odds with God's Kingdom. It is the Kingdom of God at work within our lives building the Lord's kingdom and not our own. The kingdom of God has room for every living person on earth. We just have to get that idea into our hearts and remove ourselves from persistently trying to be the front runner of all humanity.

I think that can happen by asking God where we fit in His kingdom to bring about the blessing God has planned for our lives. I sometimes find myself striving for acceptance from God, yet He has accepted me in Christ. I think the striving will stop when we realize that our stories have been written by God and that the end is truly happy, blessed, joyful, and fulfilled forever and ever. Psalm 139:16 **You saw me before I was born. Every day of my life was recorded in your book. Every moment was laid out before a single day had passed.**

We just have to rest in the fact that we, who

133

have accepted God's eternal gift, are the apple of His eye. We also have to believe the story that God is writing about us is the best story that could ever happen because God is the author and finisher of our faith. Heb. 12:2a **Looking unto Jesus the author and finisher of our faith; who for the joy that was set before him endured the cross.**

I and all my idiosyncrasies will be gone from this earth one day. What will be left behind? Only the richness of life that was invested in other people's lives will still be active on this earth and still giving God material to write my eternal story with. Yes, I can sometimes think I am very important and that I matter to me. However, I can only become fulfilled when I am securely in Him who first loved me. Father God, in Jesus name, I need and want more of you so that I can be who I truly am in you. Amen!

SIN'S HUNGER

Proverbs 30:15 The horse leach hath two daughters, crying, give, give. There are three things that are never satisfied, yea, four things say not, It is enough.

The machinations of the devil and his strategy to destroy our soul will never stop on this side of life. Satan is literally hell-bent on causing the most amount of damage, heartbreak, and destruction in the short time he has left. God put a fire in Satan that is consuming him toward overwhelming burnout. Eze. 28:18 **By the multitude of your iniquities, In the unrighteousness of your trade you profaned your sanctuaries. Therefore I have brought fire from the midst of you; It has consumed you, and I have turned you to ashes on the earth In the eyes of all who see you.**

The devil is fighting a war on two fronts;

one within himself, and the church of the Lord on the other. There is no rest or peace for our enemy as he is being consumed by God's power from within and without. Isa. 48:22 **"There is no peace," says the LORD, "for the wicked."**

The weapon most used to distract us from the love of God is the pleasures of sin for a season. Sin is fun. However, sin is only fun for a while then it takes its pound of flesh out of its victims through addictions, obsessions, debilitating anxiety, and unnatural cravings. The result of sin can leave people screaming for a fix to take away the pain that once was a pleasurable time of fun and entertainment.

The enemy's strategy is to then turn those who have submitted continually into a recidivist, going back to the scene of the crime so to speak. Many people in this day and age have forgotten that the wages of sin is still death. Rom. 6:23 **For the wages of sin is death, but the gift of God is eternal life in Christ Jesus our Lord.**

Sin's personality is that of a mugger waiting

for its chance to rob and kill you. God explains this concept to Cain because of the way Cain was responding to God's command. Cain was putting himself in harm's way of sin's effect and was vulnerable to sin's destruction. Gen. 4:7 **You will be accepted if you do what is right. But if you refuse to do what is right, then watch out! Sin is crouching at the door, eager to control you. But you must subdue it and be its master.**

God says we have to control sin or it will control us. Rom. 6:12 **Let not sin therefore reign in your mortal body, that ye should obey it in the lusts thereof.** Sin will always be crying out loud to give it more and more; similarly to the constant use of a horse leach on the back of a horse. Prov. 30:15a **The horse leach hath two daughters, crying, give, give.** The flesh of man craves fresh erotic images so to speak, but they end up the same old let down because sin, death, and destruction are not gracious to our life seeking souls.

Sin is hungry and is not prejudiced with whom it destroys. From innocent children to the dying elderly, sin craves victims no matter the social status or title a person has beside their name. Sin's hunger is insatiable. Ask anyone strongly addicted to any substance if there is a temptation to do anything, including sin, to get the momentary pleasure back? Sin is as hungry for the sinner as the sinner is for the satisfaction within the sin. James 1:15 **These desires give birth to sinful actions. And when sin is allowed to grow, it gives birth to death.** It is a lose-lose situation where only sin wins.

The good news is that Jesus conquered sin and death at the cross. Only His sacrifice and resurrection power can help any sinner overcome sin. You have to want to crush sin's hunger and get a real victory for your life. It cannot be a comme ci, comme ça attitude.

Faith in the blood of Jesus and the work of the cross will set anyone free from the power of sin and death. That is a promise from God to all mankind. We just have to receive the gift of life that has been offered once and for all. 1 Pet. 3:18 **Christ suffered for our sins once for all time. He never sinned, but he died for sinners to bring you safely home to God. He suffered physical death, but he was raised to life in the Spirit.**

GRASPING AT STRAWS

Proverbs 29:25 The fear of man brings a snare: but whoso puts his trust in the LORD shall be safe.

We can sometimes feel the unfairness of life's events or experience the momentarily unjust situations we find ourselves in. When we start grasping at spiritual straws, so to speak, we tend to pull out some old spiritual formula that worked by faith in the past but now has lost the same delivering impact we thought it should have.

Becoming overwhelmed with uncertainty and not able to hear God's voice for the noise our thoughts are making, we become desperate and grasp at any spiritual relief similar to grabbing a pain medication for the throbbing pain. Our souls sometimes forget that relationship with the Lord is a day by day

140

involvement from a personal point of the heart. Our thoughts and love toward Him are renewed every morning as God works and continually renews His love and covenant with us. Lam. 3:22 **Because of the LORD's great love we are not consumed, for his compassions never fail. 23 They are new every morning; great is your faithfulness.**

Our love relationship with the Lord is a growing, maturing, and a living force of personal involvement. It is not some formula acted upon to invoke the blessing and the favor of God. He is not some talisman or lucky-charm we call on or rub when times are hard. He is a loving God who loves us with a full and pure heart. Isa. 54:10 **"Though the mountains be shaken and the hills be removed, yet my unfailing love for you will not be shaken nor my covenant of peace be removed," says the LORD, who has compassion on you.**

The dangers of treating God like a dispensing machine for personal gain can cause us to become ungrateful, unloving, and callous of heart. Forgetting our intimacy with God may put us in a position of ungratefulness and desperately grasping for any kind of deliverance.

Moses was under pressure to meet the needs and resolve the complaints of the Israelites. The people were thirsty and needed water as they had once before in the desert. Ex. 17:6 **Behold, I will stand before thee there upon the rock in Horeb; and thou shalt smite the rock, and there shall come water out of it, that the people may drink. And Moses did so in the sight of the elders of Israel.** God had instructed Moses at that time to smite the rock and the miracle of water came forth for the thirsty crowd and their animals.

Here they were again, in another place and time, needing water and complaining as loudly as before. God instructed Moses to speak to the rock to bring about the miracle provision of water for the people. Num. 20:8 **Take the rod, and gather thou the assembly together, thou, and Aaron thy brother, and**

142

**speak ye unto the rock before their eyes;
and it shall give forth his water, and thou
shalt bring forth to them water out of the
rock: so thou shalt give the congregation
and their beasts drink.**

Moses was obviously fed up with the
complaints of the people and maybe the
pressures of leadership. His reaction in calling
the people rebels was personal and expressed
frustration and grasping for answers. Num.
20:10 **And Moses and Aaron gathered the
congregation together before the rock,
and he said unto them, Hear now, ye
rebels; must we fetch you water out of this
rock?**

Moses thought the old method or formula
per se would be good enough to bring about a
repeat performance, but it cost him his peace
and destiny. Num. 20:11 **And Moses lifted
up his hand, and with his rod he smote
the rock twice: and the water came out
abundantly, and the congregation drank,
and their beasts also. 12 And the LORD
spake unto Moses and Aaron, Because ye**

believed me not, to sanctify me in the eyes of the children of Israel, therefore ye shall not bring this congregation into the land which I have given them.

Ouch! That was not the result to a life of ministry Moses was looking for. God said, "Speak to the rock," but Moses smote the rock twice. Moses was not in obedience to the word of instruction God had given him and the result cost him dearly. Why did God let the water flow, even though Moses did not do what God said? I don't know, but what I do know is that God is faithful when I am not. Moses was grasping at straws and allowed the circumstances of his personal life to weaken his ability to be at peace within his own relationship with the Lord. Moses was focused on the rebellion of the people and how it affected him personally, rather than the grace of God.

Are you grasping at straws right now? Are you dealing with something too great for you to carry? Then grasp the foot of the solid cross that does not waver in its ability to

144

deliver our souls from any onslaught that comes our way. The bloodstained cross is where we met Jesus our Lord. It was the power that saved us and still is the power that will bring us through the murkiness of life's troubles. 1 Cor. 1:18 **For the message of the cross is foolishness to those who are perishing, but to us who are being saved it is the power of God.**

Grasping at straws or a religious formula will lead to a letdown. However, grabbing and holding on tight to the cross leads to the heart of God where we are affirmed as His beloved. Let us use our strength to wrap our arms around the one who conquered the cross. He will never disappoint our eternal souls and lives. In Jesus name!

MUCH MORE

Proverbs 15:11: Death and Destruction are before the LORD - how much more the hearts of humans!

Everything about God is much more. He has always been and will always be that way because of His infinite nature. We humans sometimes think we can come up with grandiose ideas or intelligent thought that is bigger and better than God's way of thinking, but there is always much more in God because He knows everything and intimately knows our hearts.

Some people think, "If I can just do enough to get by in life and maybe make it to some kind of place of reward, it should be good enough." However, God is thinking much more as He wants us all saved and justified within a full relationship in Him. Rom. 5:9 **Much more then, being now**

justified by his blood, we shall be saved from wrath through him. God is always so much more. Human beings are often ready to settle where they are, but God wants us to move forward toward much more in Him.

I heard a geologist say, "The reason rivers are crooked is that water makes its way through land, rock, and field, finding the least amount of resistance to make its way to the ocean." I see this same trait in the human condition. A lot of people do the same thing in life as they meander their way through life looking for the least amount of resistance and never grow to their full potential, thus becoming crooked in character and purpose.

When God wants to stretch the capacity of our heart, we pull back and coast along. We don't rise to the potential God has put within us. I'm not saying this is a law, but only a personal observation. God has much more for us than just existing and grazing our way through an insipid life. He is the God of more than enough. He is the God who gives us our heart's desires and a healthy desire for much more of what God has for us. Psalm 20:4 **May He give you the desire of your heart and make all your plans succeed.**

I have a good friend, Miss Carolyn. Nothing irks her more than seeing someone with a Godly gift and inspired potential floundering away with no purpose, wasting their time and lives by not using what God has given them for the kingdom of God. Sometimes Carolyn turns a few shades of red, not out of anger, but rather bewildering frustration at the lack of effort being put forth by a gifted person in God.

She will say with emphasis, "You have to take these gifts you have been given by God and be intentional with what you have. You cannot keep using the same old worn-out excuses you have been using for years to not get more of God. You have gifts. You have potential. You must be intentional with your faith!" I have to agree with her. There is so much more that God has for us. However, a lazy soul and spirit will not have the capacity to receive the much more God has stored up

148

for their lives.

We sometimes feel like our faith walk is a struggle and a battle. Well, it is, because it is a growing state of being every moment of the day. We were saved and we are being saved and we will be saved. This is a living, thriving, God activated life-giving force going on in us twenty-four-seven every day of our lives. The trial of our faith brings out the much more needed in us, and the much more coming from God to us. 1 Pet. 1:7 **That the trial of your faith, being much more precious than of gold that perishes, though it be tried with fire, might be found unto praise and honour and glory at the appearing of Jesus Christ.**

We can ask God with confidence for much more of Him to be revealed in us. We can ask for more because God has much more than we could even ask or think. Eph. 3:20 **Now unto him that is able to do exceeding abundantly above all that we ask or think, according to the power that works in us.** Let's stop fretting and start praying for much

149

more in our lives so we can be and do what God intended us to accomplish while we are on His green earth. As Carolyn says, "Be more intentional and the blessings will flow." Amen.

WHEN HELPING HURTS

Proverbs 9:10 The fear of the LORD is the beginning of wisdom: and the knowledge of the holy is understanding.

Sometimes it seems that helping just does not work. We put ourselves out there for the good of the people and the blessing of the needy because God has asked us to do it. Then we get the love that was intended for the unloved thrown back in our faces.

Have you ever come to the end of what was once a good idea of God's love extended, only to find out that it had turned into a rubbish heap? The entire work just came crashing down with no natural way of rescuing it. We stand there perplexed, wounded, and scared wondering if we had ever heard from God in the first place.

Most certainly during those times our pride

151

is festering and wanting some kind of salve to take away the pain of loss and failure. The word tells us not to get discouraged because the battle is won in the heavens and over a period of time. Gal. 6:9 **And let us not be weary in well doing: for in due season we shall reap, if we faint not.**

The keywords in this verse is "If we faint not." The martyrs throughout history did not see the result of their hard work and their life-giving sacrifices, but they continued in the pursuit of what God had called them to do so that we could have the freedom to own and digest the written word of God.

Sometimes it seems that we can't win. Our efforts are just going to waste. David found himself in this predicament. He had been helping defend the land of King Achish and suddenly his efforts were disregarded by politics. 1 Sam. 29:3 **Then said the princes of the Philistines, What do these Hebrews here? And Achish said unto the princes of the Philistines, Is not this David, the servant of Saul the king of Israel, which**

hath been with me these days, or these years, and I have found no fault in him since he fell unto me unto this day? At this point, David and his men return home only to find out that their own families have been taken into slavery. 1 Sam. 30:3 **So David and his men came to the city, and, behold, it was burned with fire; and their wives, and their sons, and their daughters, were taken captives.**

I don't know about you, but these events would have amounted to a very bad day for me. I would start wondering if I had heard from God concerning the call in my life. Of course the people want retribution, and it is normally the leader that will get the blunt end of the anger. 1 Sam. 30:6 **And David was greatly distressed; for the people spake of stoning him, because the soul of all the people was grieved, every man for his sons and for his daughters: but David encouraged himself in the LORD his God.**

David asks the Lord whether he is to go

after his family and the families of his men. God says, "Go!" 1 Sam. 30:8 **And David enquired at the LORD, saying, Shall I pursue after this troop? shall I overtake them? And he answered him, Pursue: for thou shalt surely overtake them, and without fail recover all.** The word that David got from God is fulfilled. He gets all his family and goods back, plus the goods of the invaders. 1 Sam. 30:17 **And David smote them from the twilight even unto the evening of the next day: and there escaped not a man of them, save four hundred young men, which rode upon camels, and fled.**

Did David go through a hard time, and did it seem all was lost? Yes, just like the times we have suffered and there was no light at the end of the tunnel. The Lord admonishes us to stay the course in faith, through Christ, and the result is that wisdom and understanding will come from God who we serve.

We do not always get the answers to why certain things happen, but if our hearts and

154

eyes are on the Lord Jesus we will get through all the situations that life throws at us. Prov. 9:10 **The fear of the LORD is the beginning of wisdom: and the knowledge of the holy is understanding.**

We will get hurt leaving our hearts out there where people will sometimes trample all over it. We can be overlooked and never thanked for what we sacrifice in the name of our Lord, but God remembers every little thing we do in His name. Matt. 10:42 **And whosoever shall give to drink unto one of these little ones a cup of cold water only in the name of a disciple, verily I say unto you, he shall in no wise lose his reward.**

Our example is Christ the Lord. When Jesus hung on the cross for the sins of the entire world, it seemed that the devil had won by provoking deicide. To the apostles and the followers of Jesus, it looked like the salvation project Jesus had started was over and all was lost. However, God had a victorious plan that resurrected Jesus from the grave and destroyed the works of the devil while enforcing the salvation plan for all mankind.

What a turn around that was and still is. We have this same resurrection power within our hearts and souls and nothing is going to stop the plan of God in our lives if we keep going, even when helping hurts. Rom. 8:37 **Nay, in all these things we are more than conquerors through him that loved us.** Kenneth Copeland said, "Faithfulness grows out of saying 'yes' to God." May saying yes to our God be on our lips when He calls. Blessings to us all.

NIGHT THOUGHTS

Proverbs 3:24 When you lie down, you will not be afraid; you will lie down, and your sleep will be pleasant.

Psalm 16:7 **I will bless the LORD who counsels me —even at night when my thoughts trouble me.**

Everybody has them - night thoughts. The thoughts that float their way into our thinking just before sleep takes us under, hopefully into a night of rest. Those thoughts that come to either please or disturb our soul. Thoughts that hover in that void just before sleep. That place of uncertainty where we wonder what eternity holds. We are utterly alone with our thoughts. If we have a clean conscience, then sleep comes easy. Prov. 3:24 **When you lie down, you will not be afraid; you will lie down, and your sleep will be pleasant.**

However, if we don't have a clean

conscience or a blessed assurance, then the questions that dog our mind will last into the night saying, "Who am I? What am I? Why am I? Have I done the right things? What will happen to me when I die? Where will I go when I die? Why can't I sleep? Why is this happening to me?" An endless night of night thoughts chirping away at our rest.

God uses our sleep time to help us stay the course and keep the plans God has sown into our lives. Job 33:15 **In a dream, in a vision of the night, when deep sleep falls upon men, in slumberings upon the bed; 16 then He opens the ears of men, and seals their instruction, 17 that he may withdraw man from his purpose, and hide pride from man.**

I believe God comes to us while we sleep and seals instructions for our life within us so we cannot argue with Him. Otherwise, there would be no end to the "Why Lord?" in everything God would say to us. This way we can clean up and repent of what our conscience is showing us because God's word is at work within us.

Those who choose to be their own god will wrestle with night thoughts. They will have rehearsed the justifications they have used to do the things they did in selfishness or anger, no matter who was hurt or destroyed. Rationalization and excuse-ology 101 are the gymnastics going on in the hearts and minds of these sleepless souls. Isa. 57:20 **But the wicked are like the troubled sea, when it cannot rest, whose waters cast up mire and dirt. 21 There is no peace, saith my God, to the wicked.** Night thoughts haunt the soul and give no rest because there is always a time of reckoning in our lives, and just before sleep is the time all of life's noises have been shut off.

The quietness before sleep is the only time we are finally lying still. Then like a rising fog in the valley of doubt, thoughts come one by one to be judged and ranked in the order of importance of God's word. God has given us a conscience. It is either clean with the grace of God's love or sullied with self-righteousness which produces fears, uncertainty, and sometimes terror. Psalm 73:19 **How are they brought into desolation, as in a moment, they are utterly consumed with terrors.**

A clean and hope-filled conscience will be rewarded with a sleep from God that is truly restful, bringing health and peace to our whole lives. Psalm 4:8 **I will both lay me down in peace, and sleep: for thou, LORD, only makes me dwell in safety.** Our night thoughts will be thoughts of peace and affirmation of God's love for us. We will know that we know God is for us.

When was the last time you rested in God and slept the sleep of the innocent? Think of God's goodness and thank Him for it. Come to Him if you are in need of rest. Matt. 11:28 **Come to me, all of you who are weary and burdened, and I will give you rest.** Rest and peace be in you. Amen.

PAINFULLY PAINFUL

Proverbs 20:30 Sometimes it takes a painful experience to make us change our ways.

Laurell K. Hamilton stated, "There are wounds that never show on the body that are deeper and more hurtful than anything that bleeds."

Pain comes in all forms. It can cripple a body, confuse a mind, and crush a soul. It can make us feel like we are the only person on earth. It can be a cruel teacher if we do not hear and respond to the lesson. Happiness does not create scars; it normally creates memories and smiles, but pain can deliver scars of all kinds.

Pain is hard to live, work, and think with. In many cases, chronic pain sufferers end up existing, rather than living. Pain consumes the total strength of their mind and body while they try to get work done. Some people have to endure excruciating migraine headaches, while some fight throbbing fiery gout in their knees and toes. There is crippling pain of the numerous arthritics, plus the burning pain of cancers which are all screaming for relief. Painful seizing back spasms are described as being whipped and lashed with the cat of nine tails. No wonder so many self-medicate to the point of numbness. All they want is to alleviate the constant pain they are living with - even if it is just for a day.

I could not imagine having to suffer or endure pain on the levels or the length of time some people have to exist in. I have only had to deal with gout on a few occasions. The fiery throbbing pain could quickly be pharmaceutically dealt with and eventually controlled through diet. I am fortunate and grateful that there was pain relief for me. However, for some people, pain is their default setting in life.

I cannot fathom the pain the mentally ill have to live through. Psalm 69:3 **I am worn**

out from calling for help, and my throat is aching. I have strained my eyes, looking for your help. My heart does not fully understand the emotional soul-wrenching grief paraplegics, war crime victims, or street drug-addicts have to fight through every day. Pain is in abundance on all levels and is not prejudiced as to who it attacks. Who will deliver us from all this pain? The Lord is able to help us overcome the pain in this world.

Jesus was acquainted with pain. Isa. 53:4a **But it was our pain he took, and our diseases were put on him.** He suffered pain on all the same levels we have to deal with in life. Jesus was rejected, betrayed, maligned, and beaten before he was crucified. He suffered in great anguishing in the garden of Gethsemane where He sweat blood. He has made a way for us to give Him our grief, sorrow, anxiety, and suffering of the mind. Jesus has opened the door for healing for us in this world. He gave Himself as a sacrifice so that we could overcome all the pain sin brought into this fallen world.

The Lord Jesus, while being crucified, was racked with pain and convulsed through the torture of the cross. Yet in those unbearable moments, He was able to say, "Father, forgive them." Luke 23:34 **Jesus kept saying, "Father, forgive them, because they don't know what they're doing." Then they divided his clothes among them by throwing dice.** Because of the finished work of the cross, faith gives us access to healing every part of our lives. 1 Pet. 2:24 **He personally carried our sins in his body on the cross so that we can be dead to sin and live for what is right. By his wounds you are healed.**

There is so much pain and suffering in this world that has been brought on by sinful men. Jesus, through His blood, has given us salvation and healing if we want it. It cannot be earned. It must be received by faith. We put our faith in the perfect and acceptable sacrifice that God the Father gave us. Jesus is that gift. Matt. 11:28 **Then Jesus said, "Come to me, all of you who are weary** and carry heavy burdens, and I will give you rest."

In many cases, pain is a hard fact in people's lives, but the truth is that Jesus is the healer and can be approached so that we may touch the hem of His garment and be made whole. Nahum 1:7 **The LORD is good, a strong hold in the day of trouble; and he knows them that trust in him.** Trusting in the Lord and the finished work of the cross is the beginning of our healing. Let us receive all the blessings God has for us through Christ. Let us remember, Jesus took all our pain with Him to the cross. In Jesus name, we ask for healing. Psalm 69:29 **But as for me - poor and in pain - let your salvation protect me, God.** Amen.

DARKNESS BLEEDS

Proverbs 3:30 Don't accuse anyone without cause, when he has done you no harm.

Mēdeia is an ancient Greek tragedy written by Euripides. A quote from that story says, "Hate is a bottomless cup; I will pour and pour". If this were written today, it could easily have been inspired by the endless amounts of hate that trolls spew out regularly on social media.

The gluttonous feeding frenzy that occurs when someone falters in public service, or life in general, creates an explosion of vicious opinions on social media - regardless of the accusations being true or false. Like voracious piranhas devouring a wounded and bleeding carcass within seconds of the first bite, these trolls devour the innocence or guilt of people's lives at the same rate of

166

consumption. They don't stop long enough to consider that they may be out of line with their hateful slanders. Psalm 53:4 **Will those who do evil never learn? They eat up my people like bread and wouldn't think of praying to God.**

This kind of darkness of heart bleeds into our social fabric, staining whatever it touches with hateful anger. It causes a mob mentality and a cruel outlook on anything and everything pure and honest. John 8:59 **Therefore they took up stones, that they might cast at Him; but Jesus hid Himself, and went forth out of the temple.**

Let's face it. There is nothing new here. There has always been slander. Even if you do not accept that Jesus is Lord, you do have to admit He was an honest and forthright man. Yet people or the trolls of His day wanted to stone Jesus because of things He had said. The difference of opinions about Jesus was as diverse then as they are now. John 9:16 **Some of the Pharisees said, "This man is not from God, for he does not keep the**

Sabbath." But others said, "How can a man who is a sinner do such signs?" And there was a division among them.

Character assassination starts off with belittling snide remarks and derogatory comments. However, history shows us that it does not take long before lynch mobs and burnings become acceptable actions for the venting of indignant rage. We are the Lord's hand extended in this dark world. Grace must be the balm anointing our hands as we reach out in the love of God. We are to hand out the bread of life to those who are hungry for righteousness and offer the salt that causes a thirst for the love of God.

Where do we get the notion that we have the right to comment and cast hard judgments on anything another person says or does? I thought judgment was the Holy Spirit's job. John 16:8 **The Spirit will come and show the people of this world the truth about sin and God's justice and the judgment.** There is enough darkness and shadows around us without us creating more. We are

168

supposed to be the light of the world. We are to shed that light through love and mercy, not condemnation and slander. Prov. 3:30 **Don't accuse anyone without cause, when he has done you no harm.**

Signs throughout British Columbia say, "Do not feed the wildlife." Well, don't feed the trolls or give them the assurance that what they are saying and doing is alright. Let us bring back to society and each other a loving respect that is birthed in the knowledge of God and His love for us. Satan is a troll with a bottomless cup of hate. He slanders and stands accusing the saints with lies and innuendo, making it up as he goes along. Zech. 3:1 **Then he showed me Joshua the high priest standing before the angel of the LORD, and Satan standing at his right hand to accuse him.**

The Lord Jesus, on the other hand, makes intercession for us and defends our lives with His blood and righteousness. Rom. 8:34b **Christ Jesus is the one who died, but even more, has been raised; he also is at the**

169

right hand of God and intercedes for us.
He continually blesses us so that we can go
out and do no harm to those Jesus died for.

Before you get ready to jump in and slander
someone who is in the headlines of all the
media outlets, ask yourself who it is that is
promoting the barrage of juicy tidbits. Prov.
18:8 **A gossip's words are like choice food
that goes down to one's innermost being.**
Remember who you are! Darkness may bleed,
but you are the light of the world. Matt. 5:14
**You are the light of the world - like a city
on a hilltop that cannot be hidden.**
Blessings and peace to you.

Notes:

PART FOUR
GOING DEEPER BY FAITH

Philippians 4:13 **I can do all things through Christ who strengthens me.** *We all have to walk farther and deeper into our God-given faith. We can all do better by His grace. We just have to want it.*

KISS: KEEP IT SIMPLE SAINTS

Proverbs 14:25 A true witness delivers souls: but a deceitful witness speaks lies.

I had the opportunity to lead a work friend to the Lord during a long six-hour drive. I did not know I had led him to Christ until a few days later. He phoned me to thank me for my time and words of wisdom that helped him make this miraculous decision in his life.

Throughout the road trip, I had been able to expound the Scriptures and answer almost all of his questions concerning Christ the Lord, eternity with God versus eternity in hell, and a personal relationship with Jesus versus being religious. With joy in his heart, he said that it was something I had said during our drive that caused him to ask Jesus into his heart to be his Lord.

My mind was racing over that long car ride.

I was trying to remember the apologetics that brought such a transformation. What was the great spiritual nugget that had been spoken and resulted in such a miracle that even the angels rejoice in heaven? Luke 15:10 **Likewise, I say unto you, there is joy in the presence of the angels of God over one sinner that repents**.

Well, I was surprised at what he said. He said, "It's when you said, 'It was dumb to go to hell if you do not have to.'" There it is, saints, wisdom personified. How simple a word God used to change a heart for eternity.

I was reading in the book of Acts the simple declaration given to the people of the day for a reason to believe in Christ as Savior. Acts 10:38 **How God anointed Jesus of Nazareth with the Holy Ghost and with power: who went about doing good, and healing all that were oppressed of the devil; for God was with him.**

How simple and uncomplicated the argument for receiving Jesus as Lord. Jesus went about doing good and healing all. This was a foundation of belief that could be trusted. Jesus was a true witness who delivered souls. Jesus Himself makes a similar statement when confronting the hypocrisy of the leaders of the day. John 10:37 **If I do not the works of my Father, believe me not.** 38 **But if I do, though ye believe not me, believe the works: that ye may know, and believe, that the Father is in me, and I in him.**

The religious leaders whom Jesus was trying to wake-up in their spirits had complicated the way to God to the point of ridiculousness and great difficulty. They had created laws for the laws that no longer worked. As Thomas Erskine of Linlathen says, "Those who make religion their god will not have God for their religion." Jesus did the will of the Father and the result was Mark 7:37 **And were beyond measure astonished, saying, He hath done all things well: he makes both the deaf to hear, and the dumb to speak.**

For all of the Christians who have been praying and believing for their lost loved ones,

176

I say keep praying. Keep your answers simple when they ask you questions about Christianity and the Lord.

I was once approached by a man and he said, "I heard you were once an alcoholic and that Jesus set you free."

I said, "This is true."

He said, "Can I have this in my life?"

I said, "Yes."

He said, "Now?"

I said, "Yes, we can pray and you can ask Jesus to come into your life right now to help you with your addiction."

We did pray and he did receive Jesus as his Lord. Now, I am convinced that it was the prayers of everyone else who had been praying for this man to be saved. I happened to be there to help bring him home to Christ. John 4:38 **I sent you to reap that whereon ye bestowed no labour: other men laboured, and ye are entered into their labours.**

There are times of difficulty and apparent hopelessness during our desire to see our family and friends saved, but as found in Prov. 14:25 **A true witness delivers souls: but a deceitful witness speaks lies.** Our lives will not lie if we stay true to our Lord.

We have the Holy Spirit guiding us toward our expected end and the glorification of Jesus our Lord. Keep it simple saints. We will be blessed. Father, in Jesus name, help us to be your hand extended and represent you with the heart of Jesus and may it be said of us that "we did all things well."

AN ANOINTED MAN

Proverbs 21:22 A wise man scales the city of the mighty and brings down the stronghold in which they trust.

What can an anointed man do? It is incredible what God can do with an ordinary man who is walking in God's favor and anointing. An anointed man can scale the city of the mighty and bring down the stronghold. Samson was a judge in Israel. When the Holy Spirit came upon him, he defeated the Philistines. Judges 15:14 **And when he came unto Lehi, the Philistines shouted against him: and the Spirit of the LORD came mightily upon him, and the cords that were upon his arms became as flax that was burnt with fire, and his bands loosed from off his hands.15 And he found a new jawbone of an ass, and put forth his hand, and took it, and slew a thousand men**

therewith.

Think about it. The jawbone of a donkey was lying there in the dust. With that jawbone, Samson kills a thousand men. Most importantly, the power of the Holy Spirit's anointing was upon him. Samson took a most unlikely thing and with it destroyed those who tied him up, the persecutors of Israel. What is in your grasp right now that could be used to defeat the enemy of your soul?

An anointed man can make the bitter things of life sweet and victorious. Elisha was approached by the men of Jericho who said the land was barren and the water was not good. Elisha, with the anointing of God in his life, took some salt and put it in the water and healed the water. 2 Kings 2:20 **And he said, Bring me a new cruse, and put salt therein. And they brought it to him. 21 And he went forth unto the spring of the waters, and cast the salt in there, and said, Thus saith the LORD, I have healed these waters; there shall not be from thence any more death or barren land.**

180

Wow, an anointed man with the Holy Spirit was able to heal the land and give the people healthy drinking water. Elisha was able to take a bitter situation and make it a blessing for all. What could you do with the anointing of God in your life? What bitterness out there in the world could you bring life to and bring a healing touch to? As Jesus said in Matt. 5:13a **You are the salt of the earth.**

An anointed man with God's direction can heal the sick and cast out devils tormenting people's lives. Paul had the favor of God. He ministered healing by sending forth healing with a handkerchief. The handkerchief was laid on a sick person who would be healed. Acts 19:11 **And God was doing extraordinary miracles by the hands of Paul,12 When handkerchiefs or aprons that had merely touched his skin were placed on sick people, they were healed of their diseases, and evil spirits were expelled.**

What can an anointed man of God do? With God in control, there is plenty an anointed man can do. Nothing is impossible for those who believe God and the love He has for us. Matt. 19:26 **Jesus looked at them intently and said, "Humanly speaking, it is impossible. But with God everything is possible."**

We all have the blessing of God's anointing available to us because of what Jesus did. The finished work of the cross has given us a gift that is beyond understanding. Christ made us, who have received Him as Lord, the temple of the Holy Spirit. We are walking containers of God's blessings and power. Jesus Christ lives within us, ministering His anointing through our lives. What an honor and blessing the Lord has given us. That is who we are, anointed man and women of God, loved and blessed by Him. With that anointing in us, we can and are able to bring down the strongholds of our life. Thank you, Lord, for your anointing.

THE LAST ENEMY

Proverbs 16:7 When a man's ways please the LORD, He makes even his enemies to be at peace with him.

My pride is ruining my testimony. I want the grace of God in my life, but I want God's judgment on my enemies' lives without mercy. Well saints, this pride will not do. In order for my enemies to be at peace with me, I must please the Lord.

God's first order of faith is in Him, and second that I love my neighbours and my enemies as myself. Mark 12:30 **And thou shalt love the Lord thy God with all thy heart, and with all thy soul, and with all thy mind, and with all thy strength: this is the first commandment. 31 And the second is like, namely this, Thou shalt love thy neighbour as thyself. There is none other commandment greater than**

these. Luke 6:27 **But I say unto you which hear, Love your enemies, do good to them which hate you.** Choices in life are most often simple, but not always easy to live out.

We read in the book of Genesis the story of Joseph who was betrayed by his brothers because of jealousy. After years of slavery and imprisonment, Joseph emerges as second-in-command only to Pharaoh himself.

Joseph's brothers came to Egypt to buy food because of a great famine in the land. Now they must deal with Joseph who is now in a position of great power and can exact revenge. However, Joseph forgives his brothers. Gen. 45:4 **And Joseph said unto his brethren, Come near to me, I pray you. And they came near. And he said, I am Joseph your brother, whom ye sold into Egypt. 5 Now therefore be not grieved, nor angry with yourselves, that ye sold me hither: for God did send me before you to preserve life.**

There was a lot for Joseph to forgive here; yet he could see that it was God who had

184

directed his life and turned everything to the good for Joseph personally. He also preserved a nation from starvation. God made his enemies to be at peace with him. Better yet, Joseph was also at peace with his enemies who were now restored brothers.

Truly the Psalmist says it right in Psalm 23:5 **You prepare a table before me in the presence of mine enemies: You anoint my head with oil; my cup runs over.** This is our portion of a full cup when we are walking in a way that pleases the Lord. We will live in peace even though there are enemies in our lives, whether they are spiritual or natural enemies. Deut. 28:7 **The LORD shall cause thine enemies that rise up against thee to be smitten before thy face: they shall come out against thee one way, and flee before thee seven ways.**

This does not mean we will never encounter problems or demonic attacks, but it means we will have the confidence in our God who will help us with the battle these protagonists bring. Deut. 20:4 **For the**

185

LORD your God is He that goes with you, to fight for you against your enemies, to save you. The fact that we are believing, by faith, that God is our ever-present-help is pleasing to God and He will go to war and fight the enemies of our lives. God will rebuke the devourer for our sakes and restore what was taken from us. 2 Kings 17:39 **But the LORD your God ye shall fear; and he shall deliver you out of the hand of all your enemies**.

The blessing of this incredible benefit from God is that we can count on the Lord to take this fight of the destruction of our enemies to the very end. Death is the last enemy we will contend within our lifetime. 1 Cor. 15:26 **The last enemy that shall be destroyed is death**. The finished work of the cross of Jesus Christ has consumed our eternal death and all the fears that come with it. The Psalmist says that we will be guided even unto death. Psalm 48:14 **For this God is our God for ever and ever: He will be our guide even unto death.**

186

We now have victory over death and will be guided through this process that can overwhelm us and cause fearful thoughts from this last enemy. The Lord encourages us not to fear this enemy because He has overcome death for us. 1 Cor. 15:55 **O death, where is thy sting? O grave, where is thy victory?**

When a man's ways please the LORD, He makes even his enemies to be at peace with him. What an amazing salvation we have that death, our last enemy, has been defeated by the cross and blood of our Lord and Savior Jesus Christ. Rev. 1:8 **I am he that lives, and was dead; and, behold, I am alive for evermore, Amen; and have the keys of hell and of death.**

Lord, we ask in Jesus name, that you continue to remind us of your powerful work that was done in our hearts and in our lives. Lord, you have saved us from the deceptions of the enemy. You, LORD, alone have defeated all our enemies - including death - and we are grateful. Amen.

HAPPY NEW RESTORATION

Proverbs 10:27 The fear of the LORD prolongs days: but the years of the wicked shall be shortened.

Yiddish saying: "If his words were a stick, you couldn't lean on it."

It's that time of the year again when people of different stripes, sizes, and beliefs make their New Year's resolutions to become a better person, or at least try to become more accomplished at something. As so often reported, these promises to self rarely come to fruition because it takes the resolve of intent, the character of heart, and the strength of will to accomplish anything of lasting worth in life.

The resolution promised to soul and character will take something more than a whimsical declaration of intent at the beginning of a new year to come about as reality. It will take fortitude and an honest desire to accomplish that which God has hidden in our deepest selves that God birthed within us and will come out at the right time in our lives. Jer. 31:33 **But this shall be the covenant that I will make with the house of Israel; After those days, says the LORD, I will put my law in their inward parts, and write it in their hearts; and will be their God, and they shall be my people.**

This character change within us will take more than a resolution, because in most cases it takes the restoration of soul and character to overcome hindrances in life. We do not just want to be seen as doing what is right in life, but actually be doing what is right regardless of whether we are seen or not.

When we live in that state of being, we will not have to wait until a new year starts to try again. We will look for restoration immediately upon noticing we are out of alignment with what God is doing in our lives. Restoration of heart and spirit will be our

189

desire. Psalm 51:12 **Restore unto me the joy of thy salvation; and uphold me with thy free spirit.** If we allow this type of honest change in our lives, then what we say and do can be counted on as reliable.

There are so many areas of our lives that need real restoration and healing. True restoration comes from the Lord who is the restorer of souls and lives. Isa. 57:18 **I have seen his ways, and will heal him: I will lead him also, and restore comforts unto him and to his mourners.** We often think we can fix our deep personal problem on our own, yet we just have to look around and see the mess the world is in to know we are failing to fix anything of worth. If we could actually fix things, would we not be in better shape as a human race? John 15:5 **I am the vine, ye are the branches: He that abides in me, and I in him, the same brings forth much fruit: for without me ye can do nothing.**

The restoration of the Lord is a good and complete work. God restores our health and the wounds of our life. Jer. 30:17a **For I will** restore health unto thee, and I will heal thee of thy wounds, saith the LORD. The Lord will restore our soul if we let him. Psalm 23:3a He restores my soul.

The Lord will restore our ability to grow and be a blessing to one another. He will restore our dignity and self-worth in Him. Joel 2:25 And I will restore to you the years that the locust hath eaten, the cankerworm, and the caterpillar, and the palmerworm, my great army which I sent among you. 26 And ye shall eat in plenty, and be satisfied, and praise the name of the LORD your God, that hath dealt wondrously with you: and my people shall never be ashamed.

Since I have a choice between restoration in Christ or fulfilling a resolution in my own strength, I will take the restoration by the hand of God because it will be done right and will accomplish a deeper and lasting work in my spirit, soul, and body. Jude 1:24 Now unto Him that is able to keep you from falling, and to present you faultless before the presence of His glory with exceeding joy.

191

This year's end brings us to a place of reflection where we look back and calculate whether we are pleased with what has transpired in our lives. The year in review per se. I am blessed that there have been some great milestones of accomplishment and blessings. I know there is room for much more from God for the coming year. So, we ask ourselves, "Did we accomplish what the Lord put in our hearts? Is there room for greater improvement of attitude and life choices?" There is in my life.

I don't think a promised resolution can pull it off for me. I believe it will take the power of the one who created me and knows me intimately to work a work deep within me to accomplish the purpose which God created me for. Psalm 139:13 **For it was You who created my inward parts; You knit me together in my mother's womb.**

This last year was definitely a year of restoration for me. I personally want to thank God for all the restoration He has done in my life. Jer. 30:17a **For I will restore health unto**

thee, and I will heal thee of thy wounds, saith the LORD. The restoration of the Lord works. I hope we all allow the Lord to restore us to a place where we can all be counted on to be a blessing in this world and life. Happy new restoration, everyone.

DEAR ANN LANDERS

Proverbs 16:23 The heart of the wise makes his mouth intelligent, and upon his lips increases learning.

Dear Ann.

I have this problem.

Every significant problem I have ever solved in my Christian life came as a result of finding the answer in the word of God, then applying my faith and many times the faith of others to the challenge or problem. Why do we wait and go looking for God, last of all, to figure out what to do about the pickle we sometimes find ourselves in? I know that it makes for good network ratings - all of the Dr. Phil type tabloid programming, but do these dumb-down servings of milky-toast psychobabble actually help anyone? I do not know. 1 Tim. 6:20 **Timothy, guard what God has entrusted to you. Avoid godless,** foolish discussions with those who oppose you with their so-called knowledge.

Grant it, if a person does not have anything other than a TV to get their souls fed, then I reckon Dr. Phil will have to do. However, if we are blood-washed children of the most high God, then we are blessed to be able to go to the Spirit of wisdom directly. James 1:5 **If any of you lack wisdom, let him ask of God, that gives to all men liberally, and upbraids not; and it shall be given him.** Thank God we have the King of kings and the Lord of lords guiding us to an expected good result on a daily and personal level. Rom. 8:31 **What shall we then say to these things? If God before us, who can be against us.**

Ann Landers stated that the majority of the letters she received asking for help had to do with fearfulness in their situation. Most often the first thing said in the bible when people had an angelic or Godly encounter was "Fear not." Isa. 41:10 **Fear thou not; for I am with thee: be not dismayed; for I am thy God: I**

will strengthen thee; yea, I will help thee; yea, I will uphold thee with the right hand of my righteousness.

The majority of our problems are fear rooted. Most of the time we keep talking about what we are afraid of. Then we keep enforcing it with our words and actions. God's inspired idea is for us to say what God says about what we are encountering and to use our faith in Christ to win the battle over the fearful thing by speaking God's anointed word. Eph. 6:17 **And take the helmet of salvation, and the sword of the Spirit, which is the word of God.**

We are to use the Word of God as our weapon of choice so that our hearts can be filled with the wisdom of God and break the yoke of bondage in our lives and the lives of others. Someone said, "The chains of habit are too light to be felt until they're too heavy to be broken." The word of God can break every bad habit and fear there is when faith in the word of God is used and believed in. We just have to start doing it, no matter how

196

awkward it seems.

We live in a negative and wounded world. All the clever and pithy sayings to help relieve the hardships in life are not faith-filled, but most often said in a deprecating humorous way. These worldly and sullied confessions keep well-meaning people stuck and struggling through life as they go along moaning words such as "Why does this always happen to me?" We physically and consciously must rise up in heart and say what God is saying about our health, wealth, and state of being in Christ our Lord.

Prov. 16:23 **The heart of the wise makes his mouth intelligent, and upon his lips increases learning.** When the word of God is proceeding from our lips, our hearts are increasing in learning what God says about our situation. If we do speak God's word by faith into our circumstances, it will not be long before we are living in the fulfillment of what God's word said is actual and true about our everyday Christian lives.

Living a blessed life will be compromised

when continual fear and unbelief are the expressed words from our lips. The word of God is the truth about our life, but we must confess it and act upon it as if fully done. Psalm 119:105 **Thy word is a lamp unto my feet, and a light unto my path.**

If we are having a difficult time obtaining wealth or paying off debt, then let us say what the Lord says about our blessing if we receive it. Deut. 28:8 **The LORD shall command the blessing upon thee in thy storehouses, and in all that thou set thine hand unto; and he shall bless thee in the land which the LORD thy God gives thee.** Luke 6:38 **Give, and it will be given to you; a good measure pressed down, shaken together, and running over will be poured into your lap. For with the measure you use, it will be measured back to you.**

If we are struggling with health problems, then let us proclaim what the word that God says is ours to receive. 3 John 1:2 **Beloved, I wish above all things that thou may**

prosper and be in health, even as thy soul prospers. 1 Pet. 2:24 **Who His own self bare our sins in His own body on the tree, that we, being dead to sins, should live unto righteousness: by whose stripes ye were healed.** Psalm 107:20 **He sent his word, and healed them, and delivered them from their destruction.**

The problems we are suffering from and trying to conquer in our lives are factual; they are real, and they exist. There is no denying that, but the truth of God's living word is more real and can overcome fact. The word of the Lord has more power and deliverance for our present reality of any situation we find ourselves in. That is the place we have to grow and mature.

Are there trials and tribulations? Yes! Are there victories and the love of God working on our behalf? Yes, and much more. So why not focus on the victory ahead and the blessing to come? God's word is righteous and eternally set for us all. Why not practice the presence of the word in our life? Don't bother

199

sending Ann Landers or any of her contemporaries a letter asking for help that will never arrive.

Let us put God's word on our lips and see the goodness of the Lord work a good work in our living souls. Amen. Isa. 55:11 **So shall my word be that goes forth out of my mouth: it shall not return unto me void, but it shall accomplish that which I please, and it shall prosper in the thing whereto I sent it.**

A LOOSE TONGUE

Proverbs 8:6 Hear; for I will speak of excellent things; and the opening of my lips shall be right things.

Loose lips sink ships was a slogan during the second world war. This expression simply said, "Unguarded talk may give useful information to the enemy." Well, Saints, this idea has not changed to this day. We have to watch what we say about others and ourselves. I know there are whole TV commercial industries dedicated to the embellished voyeurism and so-called tattletale reporting of people's indiscretions, but that does not make it right. James 3:6 **And the tongue is a fire, a world of iniquity: so is the tongue among our members, that it defiles the whole body, and sets on fire the course of nature; and it is set on fire of hell.**

How many times have you said something

that you wish you could take back, but it is never coming back. Those words are out there forever, pulsing along as amplified sound waves of your thoughts that came out too harshly, accusingly, or in unguarded anger. We can often spot this fault in others when they say something that should have been edited before it came out of their mouths, but unfortunately, we don't hear it so clearly when we speak without thought. Sng. 1:6b **They made me the keeper of the vineyards; but mine own vineyard have I not kept.**

I was listening to a minister that I greatly respect and learn easily from his gifted ability to teach. A few Sundays ago he said something that he should not have said. I know he thought what he said was funny, but it was derogatory and just not nice. I could tell as he was telling the joke he did not feel that comfortable with what he was saying, yet he said it anyway. I noticed that there was a conviction in his heart about it because he was stumbling and struggling for words for the next few sentences in order to get his

202

momentum back, but it was faltering.

The discomfort of the audience could be felt; however, it was too late to take back the words said. I think the Holy Spirit dealt with him right there and then because we could sense conviction taking place in his heart. Sometimes it is the little things said that are corrosive and gives the enemy substance to accuse us with. Sng. 2:15 **Take us the foxes, the little foxes, that spoil the vines: for our vines have tender grapes.** Yes, the little foxes spoil and ruin things.

Psalm 73:15 **If I say, I will speak thus; behold, I should offend against the generation of thy children.** Reading this scripture helps me see that the psalmist is struggling with a decision of thought. He seems to be saying, "Should I say this or not?" The psalmist is wrestling with what he perceives as God's unwillingness to enforce judgment on the unbeliever. He wants to voice his thoughts; however, he realizes that if he does vocalize what he is thinking, then the words would offend God's children.

There might be irreparable damage that will take place if the words come out. However, thank God in the next few verses he gets the illumination on the truth of the matter. Psalm 73:17 **Until I went into the sanctuary of God; then understood I their end.** There is a right time and way to say what has to be said. We just have to control the unholy rhetoric that so easily comes out of our mouths. Prov. 25:11 **A word fitly spoken is like apples of gold in pictures of silver.**

A graceful tongue is what we, as Christians, are trying to accomplish. We hopefully speak words to our friends and neighbours that build up and help fulfill the love and blessing of the Lord in their lives. I am not advocating that false platitudes and phony compliments be thrown around with an obsequious and smarmy attitude. I am talking about a genuine heartfelt leading of the Holy Spirit that expresses exactly what a person needs to hear to be lifted out of their funk, or a word that nourishes their soul onto higher ground where they meet the Lord.

204

We can do this because the Lord of glory lives within us, but we have to give the use of our tongue to the will of God to speak blessing upon blessing in this world in need of an overwhelming amount of healing. Unguarded talk may give useful information to the enemy. Guard our talk so that we can destroy the works of the enemy and be a blessing in the Kingdom of God. Matt. 6:10 **Thy kingdom come. Thy will be done in earth, as it is in heaven.** Amen!

WRITER'S BLOCK

Proverbs 3:3 Let love and faithfulness never leave you; bind them around your neck, write them on the tablet of your heart.

Writer's block: The condition of being unable to think of what to write or how to proceed with writing.

So, if a Christian cannot think of what to do next or how to proceed in his or her Christianity, is that Christian Block? Just wondering. Sometimes we just don't know what to do next, even though we have the Lord of glory living within our very beings; we just get stuck. Someone said to me, "At my age, I should have it figured out by now. I should know what to do next because I am supposed to have a lifetime of knowledge accumulated, but I just can't take the next step. I'm at a loss as to what to do."

Job was going through the same thing when he was stuck in his predicament. Job 32:7 **I thought, 'Age should speak; advanced years should teach wisdom.'** It sometimes seems like it will take forever for the tides of change to come along and deliver us from the mess or misery we find ourselves in. It might even be the stagnation of living in mediocrity that makes life seem like it has no zest to it. No, saints. We are more than earth-suits walking around in wonderment as to what will happen next. We have prospects. We have a future, and we have God. This is a winning formula in any stage of life.

God gives us a hint as to what to do when we seem to be at odds with our own sleepiness of spirit. God says, "Get rid of that writer's block by writing the vision down. Get your heart's thoughts on paper, cardboard, wood, slate or anything that can record a written word." Hab. 2:2 **And the LORD answered me, and said, Write the vision, and make it plain upon tablets, that he may run that reads it.** You will notice that

207

obedience to this word will help you become someone who is running with the word of the Lord because God says, "He may run that reads it."

We often think the vision God put in our hearts is taking too long to come to fruition; however, God says, "The time is near and not to give up on our hopes and dreams." Hab. 2:3 **This vision is for a future time. It describes the end, and it will be fulfilled. If it seems slow in coming, wait patiently, for it will surely take place. It will not be delayed.** What a profound statement: "It will not be delayed." God is in the ministry of fulfilling visions and knows how to make all things work toward our good. Rom. 8:28 **And we know that in all things God works for the good of those who love him, who have been called according to his purpose.**

Don't allow writer's block cloud the view of your awesome and mighty God who is on the throne of your heart giving life to your spirit with an all-powerful vision that only you and God can fulfill. You have to remember that you and God are a majority. What God has put in our hearts is eternal and will accomplish that which God intends.

Don't let the enemy of your soul lull you into spiritual drowsiness by reminding you of your past disappointments. No, saints, we look to the future and upon new horizons that await us in the power of our Savior and Lord Jesus. There has never been or ever will be a disappointment in Jesus. The Lord Jesus is life, joy, peace, and wonder to our souls. If the Lord be for us and with us, really, who can be against us? Rom. 8:31 **What, then, shall we say in response to these things? If God is for us, who can be against us?**

Take the time this week to write down all the blessings of the Lord that have taken place in your life this past decade and see the faithfulness of God. You will notice so many good things have happened to you and for you that you may not have enough room to record the love God has lavished upon you and your loved ones. Psalm 77:11 **I will remember the works of the LORD: surely**

I will remember thy wonders of old.

I venture to say that if you do write down all the blessings and visions fulfilled in your life, any writer's block that might have been prevalent will utterly dissipate with your memories of God's love and glory residing in your heart. Go for it. Try writing down what good things God has done for you. I dare you. I double-dog dare you.

NOTHING IS WORKING OUT

Proverbs 2:8 He keeps the paths of judgment, and preserves the way of his saints.

Have you ever had the feeling like the world was plotting against you? Nothing seems to be working out. You are sure there is some master plan that is out to get you. Jesus said, "In this world, we will have trouble." John 16:33 **I have told you these things, so that in me you may have peace. In this world you will have trouble. But take heart! I have overcome the world.** It is interesting that when things are going right, we think God is in full control; however, when things are going wrong according to our spiritual analysis, we somehow think God has lost control and we have to take over and get things right on our own.

211

I know these verses would not be found in a promise-box, but it is scripture nonetheless. Matt. 10:22 **You will be hated by everyone because of me, but the one who stands firm to the end will be saved.** In another place, the word says in John 15:18 **If the world hates you, keep in mind that it hated me first.** I'm not trying to make out as some martyr or looking for punishment, because our punishment was put on Christ at the cross and we are saved because of it.

I am saying that in all the things we go through, God is still in control. It doesn't matter whether the events are seemingly good or bad, right or wrong. God is in control of our lives. We just have to believe that God is God and is working things out for our eternal good, regardless of whether we feel things are going well or not.

There is a story of four lepers who, by reason of their leprosy alone, were having a hard life. They were also living through a severe famine in the land to the point that cannibalism had started to take place. 2 Kings

6:28 **And the king said unto her, What ails thee? And she answered, This woman said unto me, Give thy son, that we may eat him to day, and we will eat my son to morrow.** 29 **So we boiled my son, and did eat him: and I said unto her on the next day, Give thy son, that we may eat him: and she hath hid her son.**

To make matters worse, they were under siege by the Syrians. These four lepers were debating their options of death because that was all they could see for their future. 2 Kings 7:3 **And there were four leprous men at the entering in of the gate: and they said one to another, Why sit we here until we die?** 4 **If we say, We will enter into the city, then the famine is in the city, and we shall die there: and if we sit still here, we die also. Now therefore come, and let us fall unto the host of the Syrians: if they save us alive, we shall live; and if they kill us, we shall but die.** What else could go wrong? Nothing was working out for them.

With hindsight and this recorded bible

213

story, we can see the hand of God at work and in control, but these lepers could not. It looked bad, but in one day life was about to change. God had sent a sound of many armies into the camp of the Syrians and it brought fear to the point that they ran off and left everything, from food to animals, with all paraphernalia for living.

The lepers walked into an abandoned camp, feasted on the food, then realised they must share this news with the city experiencing famine. 2 Kings 7:9 **Then they said one to another, We do not well: this day is a day of good tidings, and we hold our peace: if we tarry till the morning light, some mischief will come upon us: now therefore come, that we may go and tell the king's household.**

The famine is over and the city restored. Just a few hours earlier, all that could be seen and understood was death and destruction; yet God was in control the whole time. God was preparing a victory out of a devastating situation. As starvation and fear were taking

214

their toll, I'm sure victory was the last thing in their hearts. Yet they had been given a promise that there would be food in the city the next day. 2 Kings 7:1 **Then Elisha said, Hear ye the word of the LORD; Thus saith the LORD, Tomorrow about this time shall a measure of fine flour be sold for a shekel, and two measures of barley for a shekel, in the gate of Samaria.**

How many actually believed this report? The murmuring would have been hard to avoid because the odds of survival were insurmountable. Elisha was, in essence, saying that God is in control, even though it looks and feels so bad. What are you going through that makes victory seem so out of reach? Have you become convinced that nothing is working out? Are you now so desperate that something like cannibalism (so to speak) is your only option?

No, saints, if we could have God's view of things and events, we would see that God has our victory ready and waiting for our faith to lock onto it. We need to see our situation the

215

way King David sees it. Psalm 34:19 **The righteous person may have many troubles, but the LORD delivers him from them all.** One day we'll look back on our Christian walk and we, too, will say like the Apostle Paul in 2 Tim. 3:11 **You know how much persecution and suffering I have endured. You know all about how I was persecuted in Antioch, Iconium, and Lystra - but the Lord rescued me from all of it.**

Yes, the Lord rescued me from all of it. What we often think is not working out is working in our favor and will work out a good work in Jesus name. Stay in faith, my friends. God is good.

PERPETUAL RESTORATION

Proverbs 2:7 He holds success in store for the upright, He is a shield to those whose walk is blameless.

Jeremiah 30:17a **For I will restore health unto thee, and I will heal thee of thy wounds, saith the LORD.**

Back in August of 2014, I suffered a stroke and was saved by a miracle of God's goodness. I was delivered from the destruction and after-effects that often occur after a stroke. I am so blessed in the Lord's goodness to not have suffered any ill effects of the TIA (Transient Ischemic Attack). The TIA caused me to lose control and use of my arm, tongue, facial muscles, cognitive functions, and vision. A very frightening experience, but thank God for His goodness toward me. Psalm 103:4 **Who redeems thy**

217

life from destruction; who crowns thee with loving kindness and tender mercies.

The short version and reason for the TIA is that I have Atrial Fibrillation and my heart skips a beat here and there. Norvel Hayes says, "All these different names of diseases are names given to devils by the medical establishment." Eph. 6:12 **For we wrestle not against flesh and blood, but against principalities, against powers, against the rulers of the darkness of this world, against spiritual wickedness in high places.** Thank God there is healing available for our soul, mind, and body no matter what we come up against in life.

The last few years have been a season for healing my heart. I had to make a lot of lifestyle changes that will take care of my heart that acts out in Atrial Fibrillation. I have had to put everything I know of faith into real practice and have been blessed to learn the difference between sustaining faith and delivering faith. Prov. 2:6 **For the LORD gives wisdom: out of his mouth comes**

218

knowledge and understanding. By faith in God's goodness, I've come a long way in healing my heart and am grateful for the new lease on life, plus a revised vision for life that God's word has led me in. Psalm 107:20 **He sent out his word and healed them; he rescued them from the grave.**

The lesson I have come to understand the most is that the number of my days are in God's hands. The Lord has guided me to take better care of His temple (who I am) so that I can continue to exalt the righteousness of God. Something else I've learned is what Joel Osteen said, "You were not defined by your past, you were prepared by your past." The events of the past years could have had an ill effect on my life if I had let it, but I have a mighty God who fights my battles for me and with me. 2 Chro. 20:15b **This is what the LORD says to you: 'Do not be afraid or discouraged because of this vast army. For the battle is not yours, but God's.'**

My God is able to fulfill in me what He has created me to be and do. The stroke was a knock-down, but the last few years of getting better every day and in every way has been a building up for better things to come. Oh, I've had my bad days when it looked like there were monstrous walls to overcome because health is a moving and living thing that has to be lived through. However, God's grace is sufficient and has allowed me with the right attitude to say in my heart, "I am well able through Jesus my Lord to be completely healed." Joel 3:10b **Let the weakling say, "I am strong!"** So I'm saying everyday, "I am strong!"

The word of the Lord promises that there is restoration for our lives. Through faith in God's word, we can walk out our faith to obtain the blessed promises of God for our lives. The Lord will restore our years. Joel 2:25 **And I will restore to you the years that the locust hath eaten, the cankerworm, and the caterpiller, and the palmerworm, my great army which I sent among you.** Our God will also restore our minds and souls. Psalm 23:3 **He restores my soul: he leads**

me in the paths of righteousness for his name's sake. Our heavenly Father will restore our health and the health of those who are believing with us. Isa. 57:18 **I have seen his ways, and will heal him: I will lead him also, and restore comforts unto him and to his mourners.**

Our Lord is in the ministry of restoration. He will restore our lives. Jesus will come looking for you to restore faith, assurance, and blessing if our hearts are open to Him. It says in the book of John that a blind man who had been healed by Jesus on the Sabbath had been cast out of the synagogue because of a broken law. This man had been healed and cast out because the healing he received had been done on the Sabbath. The Word says Jesus went and looked for him. Jesus searched him out to be a blessing and bring restoration to his soul and assurance of his healing. John 9:35 **Jesus heard that they had cast him out; and when he had found him, he said unto him, Dost thou believe on the Son of God?**

Saints! What a God we serve who looks for ways to restore our faith, love, and healing. So I say, "Be restored in the Lord this day!" May there be even more restoration in the years to come for my life and all who read this. Thank you, Jesus, for your goodness.

THE BEST IS YET TO COME

Proverbs 9:11 For by me thy days shall be multiplied, and the years of thy life shall be increased.

Settling for the normal hum-drum is not what God has for us in the overall plan for our lives. Should we be grateful for what we do have? Yes, absolutely, but just doing the ordinary is far below our capabilities that God has offered us in a victorious life. Victory and the ability to bring about the kingdom of God comes from a relationship with the Lord.

Stagnation is never a good place to remain while trying to find the peace of God in our lives. God is life and the Spirit of life lives and moves within our very beings through Christ our Lord. Acts 17:28a **For in him we live and move and have our being.** We can sometimes get stuck in our everyday lives,

223

wondering if anything is ever going to change. If we have a relationship with Jesus, then we can be assured that the best is yet to come.

There is a change coming that will take care of our situation. We have to be ready to move when the Spirit of the Lord says it is time to go for the blessings He has given us. 2 Cor. 6:2 **For God says, "At just the right time, I heard you. On the day of salvation, I helped you." Indeed, the "right time" is now. Today is the day of salvation.** In another place, God says in Deut. 1:6 **The LORD our God said to us at Horeb, "You have stayed long enough at this mountain."**

The Lord said to the children of Israel that it was time to move forward and take the promised land and all the challenges that come with the move led by God. The Lord was saying they had been in one place too long. The vision God gave them could only be fulfilled if they moved forward. What is God saying to you today? Is it time to take that step of faith and possess the blessing that God has

224

stored up for you and your loved ones? Is it time to open your arms wide and get ready for the blessing that you will not have room enough to contain it because the best is yet to come? Have you been stagnate in one place too long?

When Jesus was at the wedding in Cana, He instructed the servants to fill the water-pots with water. John 2:7 **Jesus saith unto them, Fill the water-pots with water. And they filled them up to the brim.** Jesus instructs the servants to give some to the governor of the feast. He tasted it and was amazed at the quality of wine and proclaims in John 2:10 **And he said to him, "Every man at the beginning sets out the good wine, and when the guests have well drunk, then the inferior. You have kept the good wine until now!"**

In essence, the Lord is telling us that we can count on the fact that it is only going to get better. The best is yet to come for our lives. Jesus is the author and finisher of our faith and He has a victory story lined up for each one of us. God is going to bring out the best for you and in you because Jesus is the Lord of your life. The mighty God of the universe does not do things in half-measures. He is ready to bless you because the best is yet to come.

Jesus has never looked for a way to cheap out on our salvation or love that He has towards us. The Lord has always been extravagant with His love and desires for us. 2 Cor. 1:20 **For no matter how many promises God has made, they are "Yes" in Christ. And so through him the "Amen" is spoken by us to the glory of God.** The Lord has always extended blessing upon blessing toward us. Why would He change now after years of walking with Him? No, saints, God is waiting for us to believe in His goodness and wants us to be ready for the blessing because the best is yet to come. Num. 23:19 **God is not a man, that he should lie; neither the son of man, that he should repent: hath he said, and shall he not do it? or hath he spoken, and shall he not**

226

make it good?

Don't try and make God some kind of chintzy CEO of a poorly run heavenly corporation. He does not think that way. He is not trying to squeeze the bottom line of our lives for a bit more love and affection as if we were His earthly minions. God is lavish and kind in His love for us, and like a loving father wants the best for his children. Isa. 55:8 **"For my thoughts are not your thoughts, neither are your ways my ways," declares the LORD.**

My brothers and sisters, be assured that our God has kept the best for you to this very day. We can all count on the fact that the best is yet to come. So I say, "Amen and amen, Father God. Bring on your lavish love and blessings you have planned for me. I am ready for your windows of heaven to pour out a blessing, because I know the best is yet to come." John 2:10 **And he said to him, "Every man at the beginning sets out the good wine, and when the guests have well drunk, then the inferior. You have kept the**

227

good wine until now!”

Notes:

PART FIVE
OUR VICTORY

Strength and victory comes after many battles, and we have been proven by fire. Hebrews 12:29 **For our God is a consuming fire.**

I AM WHOLLY LOVED

Proverbs 1:2 To know wisdom and instruction; to perceive the words of understanding.

What an amazing existence eternity has for us. We will be able, without any self-consciousness, bow before the Lord with pure honesty from our hearts. We will be so willing to worship without hindrance that the feeling will be natural. There will be no self-imposed peer pressure whatsoever. We will utterly enjoy the love that others will express to the Lord our God. We will all be filled with pure joy that we could not find during our lives. The Lord will be filling us with His goodness at all times.

The very essence of God's being will fulfill us all. Rev. 21:23 **And the city had no need of the sun, neither of the moon, to shine in it: for the glory of God did lighten it,**

and the Lamb is the light thereof. The very fact that we will be in the presence of God will not allow any negative thoughts to enter our hearts. There will be no thoughts of putting our best foot forward because we will understand that we are fully known of Him who first loved us.

We will be so willing to give ourselves to the Lord of Glory that our hearts will cry Abba Father out of God's love coming from our own existence. Deep down we all know this type of relationship exists for us in the hereafter, but how do we get a full serving of it here today? Sng. 8:7 **Many waters cannot quench love, neither can the floods drown it: if a man would give all the substance of his house for love, it would utterly be condemned.**

Some might think I am too quixotic, exceedingly idealistic. I say, "No," to that statement. I think it is possible to get a real heavenly love anointing in our lives today. We can get an understanding of God's love through His word. Prov. 1:2 **To know** wisdom and instruction; to perceive the words of understanding.

We can, with the help of the Holy Spirit, perceive God's love for us. However, this love will be found in His word as we make it part of our lives. Job 23:12b **I have esteemed the words of his mouth more than my necessary food**. After all, it is God who lived and lives in absolute love before the foundation of creation. The love relationship between the Godhead, Father, Son, and Holy Spirit was already in existence from infinity past.

This same God who is the lover of our soul loves us; therefore, the love is ours to glean from the wholeness of our well being and lives now and forever. Sometimes we hear of people who want proof that God loves us. What more can God do? He already did the ultimate sacrifice for anyone who will accept the act of God's love by faith. 1 John 4:10 **Herein is love, not that we loved God, but that he loved us, and sent his Son to be the propitiation for our sins.**

234

The word of God is God's love letter to us. From Genesis to Revelation is a record of God reaching out to mankind on every possible level. Rom. 5:8 **But God commended his love toward us, in that, while we were yet sinners, Christ died for us.**

From the beginning, God has had His hand extended toward us. Historically, however, we have shunned Him by demanding proof of His love. The proof of God's love is that He has constantly had his hand extended to us so we would take it. If God is always trying to help us and help understand Him, then what more proof is there? If we had been utterly abandoned to our sin and left for dead per-se, that would be proof that He had no love for us. God did not do that, but rather made a way for us all to live in the most loving state of love throughout eternity.

How do we get to the place where we can walk in that love of heaven here on earth? God's wisdom helps us perceive and understand His love letter to us all. When we do accept what Christ has done for us, He is not only our Lord but our friend. John 15:15 **Henceforth I call you not servants; for the servant knows not what his lord does: but I have called you friends; for all things that I have heard of my Father I have made known unto you.**

His friendship will be experienced when we accept what He did at the cross. John 15:13 **Greater love hath no man than this, that a man lay down his life for his friends.** This is what will make us all whole in the love of God. Oh, that we will be able to get a wonderful glimpse of the eternal love that is for us today and awaits us eternally as well. God is so good. Blessings of loving wholeness on us all.

SPRING CLEANING

Proverbs 25:14 Whoso boasts himself of a false gift is like clouds and wind without rain.

I was going through the small sheds that are at the back of my yard. I noticed a lot of stuff that is not used anymore and just not wanted. I started marking things to give away and stuff to throw away. As I was wondering how all this stuff had made its way into my sheds, it occurred to me that I had allowed stuff to accumulate over time.

At that moment I thought of the Lord looking at me and wanting to do the same thing I was planning: spring cleaning. God might want to do a literal spring cleaning in my heart. All this stuff that was taking up room and had no value was clogging up the space.

I could see that we Christians might have to do the same kind of spiritual inventory in our hearts. What is taking up room that is not being used for the Kingdom of God? What has become useless and of non-effect in our walk with Christ, yet we hang on to it? What have we been boasting about that is not of God, but we think it is? Have we become clouds with no rain? Is our walk in Christ becoming insipidly dry and tasteless? Hag. 1:6 **Ye have sown much, and bring in little; ye eat, but ye have not enough; ye drink, but ye are not filled with drink; ye clothe you, but there is none warm; and he that earns wages earns wages to put it into a bag with holes. 7 Thus saith the LORD of hosts; Consider your ways.**

Yes, saints, a spring cleaning of the heart is in order. How do we submit to God so that He can begin the clean up in our hearts? We get under the hot focus of God's word and obey the corrections God is pointing out. Psalm 139:23 **Search me, O God, and know my heart: try me, and know my thoughts:**

238

24 **And see if there be any wicked way in me, and lead me in the way everlasting.**

We allow God to take away the stuff that no longer brings joy or blessing to ourselves and others. We stop collecting hurts and slights that have happened to us over time. We stop boasting of accomplishments in God that are not so. We let the Holy Spirit heal our wounds that we often use as an excuse for our misbehavior and unbelief. We grow up!

We read the story of the children of Israel deciding on whether they will believe the encouraging report of Joshua and Caleb, or the discouraging report of the other ten spies. The stories told of the land being full of milk and honey are correct and the size of the fruit they bring back is visual proof, but the stuff that is in the hearts of the people of God is clogging the faith that will be needed to take the land. Num. 13:27 **And they told him, and said, We came unto the land whither thou sent us, and surely it flows with milk and honey; and this is the fruit of it.** 28 **Nevertheless the people be strong that** dwell in the land, and the cities are walled, and very great: and moreover we saw the children of Anak there.

At this point, Caleb, who is of a different spirit and courage, tries to rally the faith of the nation of Israel. Num. 13:30 **And Caleb stilled the people before Moses, and said, Let us go up at once, and possess it; for we are well able to overcome it.** The report that is chosen is the one of the ten who are full of fear. Num. 13:33 **And there we saw the giants, the sons of Anak, which come of the giants: and we were in our own sight as grasshoppers, and so we were in their sight.**

Caleb continues to present the case that God is with them and they can take the promised land. It is a promise from God who cannot lie. Caleb is trying to show these people that taking the land will build their faith and be a strength to them over time. Num. 14:9 **Only rebel not ye against the LORD, neither fear ye the people of the land; for they are bread for us: their**

240

defence is departed from them, and the LORD is with us: fear them not. Wow, what a statement Caleb makes when he says, "They are bread for us."

Caleb sees the need to overcome giants because it feeds the power of God that is within each person. That is the same thing we have in Christ. The Lord cleans us up and makes us ready to battle the giants that come our way in life so that we can look at the trials and tribulations of life as bread for us to grow up on. 2 Cor. 10:4 **For the weapons of our warfare are not carnal, but mighty through God to the pulling down of strong holds.**

We don't have to look for trials and problems, but we do not have to run from them or fear them either. The thing is, how do we overcome when we are full of stuff that is not of God? That is why we need our heart kept clean so that we see clearly what and who we are in Christ. When we speak, we are declaring words that heal and bring rain to a parched soul.

Yes, Lord, go ahead and get rid of the stuff in my heart that causes fear of the enemy. Someone said, "Blessed is the man who digs a well for which another may draw faith." May we be that man.

MEANINGFUL WORK

Proverbs 18:9 He also that is slothful in his work is brother to him that is a great waster.

Slothful! What a word to describe that person in the office who is never on time, or dependable, or even reliable for the basics. They seem to create more work than they accomplish. Payday comes around and they are the first to complain that they are not paid enough for their special talents, whatever their talents are, and then threaten to quit.

We stand there hoping they follow through on the threat, but no, they don't quit because they are a slothful person and would not be able to follow through on anything, even quitting their jobs. So they go on looking busy and accomplishing nothing of value, or ever able to find the place where they are being fulfilled with meaningful work.

The Lord wants our attitudes to be as though we work for God Himself. Eph. 6:6 **Not with eye service, as men-pleasers; but as the servants of Christ, doing the will of God from the heart; 7 With good will doing service, as to the Lord, and not to men.**

There is a lot of dissatisfaction in the workplace today because we have not seen the blessing of meaningful work in our lives. Work was ordained before the fall of man. Gen. 2:15 **And the LORD God took the man, and put him into the garden of Eden to dress it and to keep it.** Work is God's idea for man. We were created to be creative and seek out the answers and understanding to life's puzzles, queries, mysteries, and problems. Prov. 25:2 **It is the glory of God to conceal a thing: but the honour of kings is to search out a matter.**

Part of the dissatisfaction within the human condition is when work becomes a drudgery. If we are working for money only, then it will not take long before the novelty of the new

244

job will wear off and become as boring as the last job. Yes, we need money in this market economy to make a living, but we also need the satisfaction of accomplishment. In most cases that cannot be bought.

Max Asnas said, "Money is something you got to make in case you don't die." This would be funny if it were not the pathetic way we think about accomplishments and life. We are being driven by the enemy of our soul to constantly look at what we do not have, then buying stuff and lots of it.

We then realize that our job's remuneration cannot support all the payments on the stuff bought because the law of stuff is, "Stuff begets stuff." So we glare with disdain at our jobs and work environments with attitudes of fatalism, putting us in a place of complaining and ungratefulness. We then end up under the curse of labor. Gen. 3:19a **In the sweat of thy face shalt thou eat bread, till thou return unto the ground.** We surrender to working for a ruthless master whose name is "The Great Waster." Francis Bacon said,

"Money makes a good servant but a bad master."

Meaningful work will come out of a meaningful relationship with our Lord and Savior Jesus. It might sound oversimplified, but the foundation of what I am saying is true. When I am at peace with Christ, I am at peace with most of the situations that arise at work. With the Lord's help, I can overcome what comes at me throughout the work week.

The joy of the Lord is our strength. That joy will enable us to take on the challenges, rather than cower away from them. Neh. 8:10b **For this day is holy unto our Lord: neither be ye sorry; for the joy of the LORD is your strength.** Psalm 28:7 **The LORD is my strength and my shield; my heart trusted in him, and I am helped: therefore my heart greatly rejoices; and with my song will I praise him.**

We can look back in our own personal Christian history and see that to the degree our walk and relationship with Christ was strong, so was our work ethic as strong. That

246

is why when times became hard, we went through the mess as others fell by the side in despair. We still continued to tithe because the strength of our relationship in Christ was keeping everything from falling apart around us.

As some pastors like to say, "Our mess became a message, and our test became a testimony." Isa. 30:21 **And thine ears shall hear a word behind thee, saying, This is the way, walk ye in it, when ye turn to the right hand, and when ye turn to the left.**

It does not matter what type of honest work we do. If we treat the work as a call from God, and do it well, it will manifest as meaningful work and bring fulfillment in our lives. Col. 3:17 **And whatsoever ye do in word or deed, do all in the name of the Lord Jesus, giving thanks to God and the Father by him.**

When we are grateful for the work we have and take care of the work position as if it was the pearl of great price, then God will promote us and we will never be worried about being a brother to the great waster.

MOTION IS LOTION

Proverbs 31:17 She begins her work vigorously, and she strengthens her arms.

There is a new slogan among the elderly these days, "Motion is lotion." This is another way of saying, "No matter how much it hurts, keep moving." If we take this physical dynamic into our spiritual lives, we see the same principle at work. There will be battles and warfare, but with the grace of God we will have to keep moving forward to keep winning the victory Christ has given us. As we walk through the valley of dark shadows, we will have the peace of God guiding us onward. Psalm 23:4 **Yea, though I walk through the valley of the shadow of death, I will fear no evil: for thou art with me; thy rod and thy staff they comfort me.**

Moving toward God when we stumble, flinch or fall, rather than running from Him is

249

the will of God for our lives. Heb. 4:16 **Therefore we should come with boldness to the throne of grace, so that we may receive mercy and may find grace for help in time of need.** Our forward motion in life should always be toward the Lord of our creation.

We should never be afraid of God's correction and guidance no matter what we have done, because His affection for us is love. God is not an angry father waiting to backhand or bludgeon us into unconsciousness. His heart toward us is love. Sng. 2:4 **He brought me to the banquet hall, and his banner over me was love.**

We read in the book of Mark the story of a woman who had a bleeding disorder for twelve years. She wanted healing and risked public accusation and embarrassment, yet reached out and touched the hem of Jesus' garment. Mark 5:25 **Having heard about Jesus, having come in the multitude behind, she touched his garment, 26 for she kept saying, "If only I touch his**

250

clothes, I will be healed." Her faith kept her moving forward and pushing through the crowd to the point of reaching out and touching Jesus. Her body was hurting, but she kept on moving toward the Lord who could heal her. She was physically weak and had not responded to the medical treatment of the day.

This woman was at the end of her rope, but she kept her forward motion toward Jesus the healer. Are we that tenacious when we are suffering from the troubles in life? Do we keep moving toward the Lord, regardless of the crowds around us? Giving up is so easy and tempting because worldly crowds and their opinions press us on all sides. Gal. 6:9 **Let us not become weary in doing good, for at the proper time we will reap a harvest if we do not give up.**

We can often stumble and get disillusioned by the failures we cause and encounter all around us. The Apostle Paul admonishes us to stop wallowing in the failures of our past and to reach for the victory that is ahead of us.

251

Phil. 3:13 **Brethren, I do not regard myself as having laid hold of it yet; but one thing I do: forgetting what lies behind and reaching forward to what lies ahead,** 14 **I press on toward the goal for the prize of the upward call of God in Christ Jesus.** Paul is saying, "No matter how much it hurts, keep moving forward in Christ."

We may have lost a battle, but we are not losers. We may have failed at a duty or keeping a promise, but we are not failures. We are the blood-washed children of God who are growing from glory to glory in the grace of our Lord Jesus Christ. We are the Lord's army who march forward by the leading of the Holy Spirit. The lotion for our souls is the holy balm that comes from God's love that is poured out on each one of us through Jesus the Lord. Get up, dust off, and keep moving in Him who first loved us and we'll all shout the victory. Amen.

QUO VADIS

Proverbs 29:18 When people do not accept divine guidance, they run wild. But whoever obeys the law is joyful.

Quo Vadis. Where are you going?

Good question. Where are we going in this fast and ever changing world? What is our ultimate destination? How can we get there? How fast can we get there? Many are looking for the magic bullet or pill that will help them arrive at that place of satisfaction, wherever that place and regardless of the cost to soul and pocket-book.

We want more. More of what? Just more, and we want it now, packaged so we can have immediate gratification without effort of intimate or emotional connection. Another good question might be, "Where are you?" Gen. 3:9 **Then the LORD God called to Adam and said to him, "Where are you?"**

Where are you right now in this life? Where are you going. What have you done with the life God has given you so far?

Every once in a while we all come to a place of wondering where are we going. We ask ourselves this question with a sense of vague assurance. Do the things I do, and in most cases do automatically, have any worth? Do they have any spiritual, emotional, or intrinsic value? Am I living, or just existing?

We plod along in zombie like routines that seem meaningless and aimless as lost people wandering through a desert while asking, "Where am I going? What am I looking for?" At this point many people throw up their hands in surrender to the statement of "I quit, I want out of this empty existence." That's nice, but if you quit that existence, where will you go and exist differently? Prov. 29:18 **When people do not accept divine guidance, they run wild. But whoever obeys the law is joyful.**

Someone said, "A man without a vision will always return to his past." So it looks like you might end up right back in the place of your frustration. There has to be an answer and a purpose. Living has got to be more than a mortgage, car payment, and the acquiring of never-ending stuff.

The disciples of Jesus had to answer a hard life question one day when Jesus asked them if they would leave Him as the others had because of the deep doctrines He was teaching. John 6:67 **Then said Jesus unto the twelve, Will ye also go away?** 68 **Then Simon Peter answered him, Lord, to whom shall we go? thou hast the words of eternal life.** That's it, isn't it? If God asked us, "Where are you going?", we would have to say, "To you Lord. You have the answer to our eternal life."

I do not know where you are at in your walk of life right now, but God has the road map you need to get there. Yes, God has a plan for your life and He knows how to bring His plan into fruition. Many will feel hemmed in and restricted, thinking they are losing their personal rights because God is leading. That is a bald-faced lie from the enemy of your soul. Maybe that is why Jesus said the road was narrow, because not many are asking God for His directions to get to where God wants us to eventually arrive. Matt. 7:13 **Enter ye in at the strait gate: for wide is the gate, and broad is the way, that leads to destruction, and many there be which go in thereat: 14 Because strait is the gate, and narrow is the way, which leads unto life, and few there be that find it.**

Don't let the tides and winds of this world determine your final destination. Stop and smell the heavenly roses per se. Seek God with a full heart and see what He has planned for your life. You might feel like your life resembles a ride on a roller-coaster with no brake within reach. However, giving God control at this point is not too late of a decision for your life, regardless of your age.

God can fix in a day what you have ruined in a lifetime. The enemy of your soul might say that you are stuck on a highway to hell. Psalm 3:2 **Many there be which say of my soul,**

256

There is no help for him in God. Selah.
The devil is a liar. God can change our circumstances in the twinkling of an eye. We just have to want it and want it with all our heart. Jer. 29:13 **And ye shall seek me, and find me, when ye shall search for me with all your heart.**

The next time someone says to you, "Where are you going?", you can smile and start singing that old song: "♫ ♪ Well, I'm on my way to heaven. My journey gets sweeter every day.♪ Well, I'm walking with Jesus.♫ ♪ Talking with Jesus all along the way♫ ♪♫." Yup! That's where I'm headed, Saints. The Lord has the words for my life here on earth and for my eternal life. I receive them gladly. I pray the same for you. Blessings to you.

NO WORRIES MATE

Proverbs 23:29 Who hath woe? who hath sorrow? who hath contentions? who hath babbling? who hath wounds without cause? who hath redness of eyes?

There is nothing like the peace of a good night's sleep when you have gone to bed with a clean and clear conscience. No woes, sorrows, contentions, wounds, or redness of eyes, just pure joy and peace. "Is that even possible," someone might ask? Yes, it is. The word of God says in Psalm 4:8 **I will both lay me down in peace, and sleep: for thou, LORD, only makes me dwell in safety.** The best part about our peaceful sleep is that we do not have to worry because our Lord is awake, taking care of our lives and our dreams. Psalm 121:4 **Behold, he that keeps Israel shall neither slumber nor sleep.**

How many times have you gone to bed with trouble on your heart and mind, causing a restless night of tossing and turning? Was it because you went to bed with anger or unforgiveness in your heart? Eph. 4:26 **Be ye angry, and sin not: let not the sun go down upon your wrath: 27 Neither give place to the devil.** Why would the devil want you to go to bed with woes, sorrows, contentions, babbling, wounds, or redness of eyes? Because it means you have taken on the cares of the world. In the Gospel of Mark it says these cares will choke the word right out of your life. Mark 4:19 **And the cares of this world, and the deceitfulness of riches, and the lusts of other things entering in, choke the word, and it becomes unfruitful.**

We read in the book of Acts that Herod puts Peter in prison, out of spite, to gain favor with the Jewish leaders. Now Peter is in jail on Herod's whim. He is sleeping so peacefully and soundly that the angel of the Lord has to tap him with light to wake him up. Acts 12:7 **Suddenly an angel of the**

Lord appeared, and a light shone in the cell. Striking Peter on the side, he woke him up and said, "Quick, get up!" And the chains fell off his wrists. "Get dressed," the angel told him, "and put on your sandals." And he did. "Wrap your cloak around you," he told him, "and follow me."

Peter is so at ease and in a deep sleep that he has to be told to tuck himself in and strap up his sandals. This is a man with no woes, sorrows, or contentions on his mind; only the faith in the risen Lord. How do you get that type of peace and rest? How apropos that Peter would write in his epistle 1 Pet. 5:7 **Casting all your care upon him; for he cares for you.** Peter had the right idea by casting all his sorrow, grief, anxiety and suffering of the mind on the Lord because Peter knew Christ would do all those things for him.

Paul writes in Rom. 8:38 **For I am persuaded, that neither death, nor life, nor angels, nor principalities, nor powers, nor**

260

things present, nor things to come, 39 **Nor height, nor depth, nor any other creature, shall be able to separate us from the love of God, which is in Christ Jesus our Lord.** Most of Paul's Epistles are written from prison. The peace and confidence that comes from him is awe-inspiring.

Was Paul in a position to have woes, sorrows, contentions? Yes, because we know he had wounds. 2 Cor. 11:24 **Of the Jews five times received I forty stripes save one. 25 Thrice was I beaten with rods, once was I stoned, thrice I suffered shipwreck, a night and a day I have been in the deep; 26 In journeyings often, in perils of waters, in perils of robbers, in perils by mine own countrymen, in perils by the heathen, in perils in the city, in perils in the wilderness, in perils in the sea, in perils among false brethren; 27 In weariness and painfulness, in watchings often, in hunger and thirst, in fastings often, in cold and nakedness.** Did Paul have the occasion to complain? Yes, and yet he writes in 2 Cor. 4:17 **For our light affliction, which is but for a moment, works for us a far more exceeding and eternal weight of glory.** Excuse me. Light affliction! Where does that perspective of peace come from? Lord, forgive me for thinking the music was too loud during last Sunday service.

If you find yourself full of woes, sorrows, contentions, wounds, babbling, or redness of eyes, then it might be time to let the Holy Spirit, your Comforter, into your life for an attitude adjustment. Perhaps a chiropractic correction is needed to give us some spine in our walk with Christ. Less complaining and more praying so that we find our peace in Him who first loved us. As my Aussie pastor would say, "Come on mate, get up, and let's give it another go. There are no worries here, just victory when we find it." Thank you, Pastor Hannah, for what you sowed into my life.

SINCERE, BUT SINCERELY WRONG

Proverbs 12:15 The way of a fool is right in his own eyes: but he that hearkens unto counsel is wise.

In 1988 my young family and I were living in the town of Margate, Queensland, Australia. I went to the local branch of my bank to exchange some Australian money for some Canadian cash as I had done at this branch on other occasions. The new teller looked at me as if I was odd when she said with a clear and resounding voice, "Canada does not have a currency because they use the US dollar in Canada." She said, "You will have to buy US dollars."

At first I thought she was joking, but found out that she was sincere. With a louder voice she proclaimed that I was wrong in thinking that Canada had its own currency. With

263

patience I explained that the picture of the queen was on the Canadian one dollar note, the two, and twenty dollar bill with the word CANADA across the top part of the bill. I also explained that in the past I had exchanged these notes in the very branch I was in. She started to get politely angry with me for arguing with her and exclaimed that I was mistaken.

I noticed the manager of the branch walking by, so I called him to draw his attention. He came over and asked what the problem was. The teller abruptly chimed in with a loud condescending explanation saying, "This man wants to buy Canadian cash, but as I told him there is no such thing so he has to buy US dollars." The manager looked at her with a questioning look and asked her to go help someone in the back. He got the Canadian cash for me that I was asking for and apologized for the misunderstanding. I do not know what happened with the manager-teller talk afterward, but as I walked out of the branch I realized that the teller was sincere, but sincerely wrong.

There is nothing wrong with being wrong, or sincerely wrong, since that is how we often learn what is right. We mess up, learn the lesson, and we are better for it. However, to insist on being wrong and remaining that way after the truth has been clearly revealed is the action of a fool or a gainsayer. Psalm 14:1a **The fool says in his heart, "There is no God."**

Unless you are a lawyer for big tobacco, pharmacy, or agriculture, insisting on being wrong is just plain dumb. Isa. 5:20 **Woe to those who call evil good and good evil, who substitute darkness for light and light for darkness, who substitute bitter for sweet and sweet for bitter.**

The apostle Paul was a sincere and dedicated Pharisee. He was zealous for the things of God. Phil. 3:5 **Circumcised the eighth day, of the stock of Israel, of the tribe of Benjamin, an Hebrew of the Hebrews; as touching the law, a Pharisee; 6**

Concerning zeal, persecuting the church; touching the righteousness which is in the law, blameless. Paul thought by persecuting Christians, he was doing God a favor. He was sincere, but sincerely wrong. After his encounter with the Lord Jesus on his way to Damascus, the apostle Paul learns the lesson and the error he was living in. He then changed his life to follow Christ, His Lord. Phil. 3:7 **But what things were gain to me, those I counted loss for Christ.**

When we think about how the law and all that came with being a Pharisee was ingrained in Paul's heart and life, we see clearly that Paul was no fool. Once he knew the truth of the fact that Jesus was his Lord and Savior, Paul saw that he had messed-up in what he believed and repented immediately and moved forward.

Phil. 3:8 **Yes, everything else is worthless when compared with the infinite value of knowing Christ Jesus my Lord. For his sake I have discarded everything else, counting it all as garbage, so that I could**

266

gain Christ. Thank God Paul saw he had been sincerely wrong and needed to change his view of God. He then went on to be an apostle of apostles, plus by the leading of the Holy Spirit write a large portion of the New Testament.

What have we been sincerely wrong about, but have continued to foolishly argue or fight for the right to be so? What do you know in your heart of hearts you are doing that is not right, but for the sake of being right you maintain your stances and bluster? Time to give it up and let the Spirit of truth lead and guide you to being sincerely right. Jesus is Lord. That is where it starts. John 14:6 **Jesus answered, "I am the way and the truth and the life. No one comes to the Father except through me."**

Let us turn our foolish hearts over to Christ that we may be righteous, rather than just right about something. Let us use our faith to grow in the knowledge of God so that we may be a pleasure to Him. Heb. 11:6 **But without faith it is impossible to please**

267

him: for he that comes to God must believe that he is, and that he is a rewarder of them that diligently seek him. Let us be sincere about our walk of faith in our Lord and Savior Jesus.

A GOOD WORD

Proverbs 12:25 Heaviness in the heart of man makes it stoop: but a good word makes it glad.

As an interim minister who is invited to speak in churches, I sometimes hear the Christian colloquial expression, "That was a good word!" As the above proverb says, "A good word makes the heart glad." Is that all it takes to heal and bring gladness into people's lives? Praise the Lord that we have one of the answers to the world's woes. We can bring gladness of heart to this sad world by proclaiming a good word of blessing and encouragement. Too simple, you say? I double-dog dare you to try it!

Prov. 15:4a **A wholesome tongue is a tree of life.** Steven K. Scott wrote in his book *The Richest Man Who Ever Lived* that the Hebrew word for wholesome literally translates

269

"healing" or "curative." In other words, Solomon is saying that a healing tongue is a "tree of life." What a beautiful example Steven Scott gives us.

We, who walk in Christ, can bring life because our words can be a tree of life. I love this example. Because trees, of course, are not only alive, they provide life to others. We can bring good and healing words to the world around us because we are living by God's life-giving word. Psalm 107:20 **He sent his word, and healed them, and delivered them from their destructions.** God's word is intended to bring life and healing to those who need it.

So many of the hurt people we encounter on a daily basis are carrying wounds from malicious words that were carelessly thrown at them throughout their lives. The resulting pain has caused a corrosiveness of heart, resulted in different ill effects and suffering depressions of the souls. Psalm 42:5a **Why, my soul, are you so dejected? Why are you in such turmoil?**

We read the story of Hagar, the bondwoman of Abraham and Sarah. Hagar and her son Ishmael become victims of circumstance. They are thrown out of their family life by the request of Sarah. Gen. 21:10 **Wherefore she said unto Abraham, Cast out this bondwoman and her son: for the son of this bondwoman shall not be heir with my son, even with Isaac.** I am sure there were deep wounds and hurts for being treated so ruthlessly.

The castaways run out of water in the desert and are preparing to die when God comes to Hagar with kind words concerning her son. Gen. 21:17 **God heard the boy crying, and the angel of God called to Hagar from heaven and said to her, "What's wrong, Hagar? Don't be afraid, for God has heard the boy crying from the place where he is."** Words inspired by God heal and bring life to the hearts of men. God's specific words a mother wants to hear are heard - her child will be alright. Truly a good word made the heart glad.

We who know our God have the ability to inspire many lives by simply being careful of how we say things. A good word in season can change a life from disaster to victory. It can change a tense and augmentative situation from anger to a peaceful resolution. Prov. 15:1 **A soft answer turns away wrath: but grievous words stir up anger.**

We have the ability to bring healing, peace, joy, and blessing to many situations in life. We just have to want to do it. Imagine changing your environment by the kind words you speak and act upon. What a wonderful world that would be. Start by bringing a good word within your family. Try it, I double-dog dare you! Blessings, saints.

BLESSED WORDS GIVE LIFE

Proverbs 25:23 As surely as a north wind brings rain, so a gossiping tongue causes anger!

John Osteen said, "Keep your words sweet because you might have to eat them one day."

As sure as the laws of nature work all around us each and every day, so does the laws of the spoken word that proceeds from our hearts then out of our mouths. Matt. 12:34 **O generation of vipers, how can ye, being evil, speak good things? for out of the abundance of the heart the mouth speaks.** Someone might say, "Oh, I'm sorry, I didn't mean to say that in anger." Yes, you did, because it came from within your heart. That anger was there in your heart and that is what came out of your mouth. This is a law of life.

Most assuredly, apologize, but remember it was there.

What is the root of that anger? That should be the question foremost in our minds so that we can get rid of the root problem of bitterness. If the angry words of backbiting could have been curtailed in that moment of uncontrolled verbal abuse, there would not have been the damage to a soul or a relationship that blew up in a hurtful result.

How often have people wished they could have taken back the angry words that had been spoken? How often has a piece of gossip slipped through our lips to cause irreparable damage? Someone said, "Gossip is as vicious as murder; the difference is we are killing a soul rather than a body." This is why God admonishes us to speak words of blessing and honor to nurture and bring healing to relationships and set the souls of those who are hurting free from the shackles of wounding words. Prov. 25:11 **A word fitly spoken is like apples of gold in pictures of silver.**

274

We see the reaction of Michal when she sees King David dancing as the ark of God was brought back into the city of David. 2 Sam. 6:16 **And as the ark of the LORD came into the city of David, Michal Saul's daughter looked through a window, and saw king David leaping and dancing before the LORD; and she despised him in her heart.** The words that come from Michal's mouth are a result of what was in her heart. She could not disguise the anger and hatred that came forth. 2 Sam. 6:20 **Then David returned to bless his household. And Michal the daughter of Saul came out to meet David, and said, How glorious was the king of Israel to day, who uncovered himself to day in the eyes of the handmaids of his servants, as one of the vain fellows shamelessly uncovers himself!**

It is not recorded in the description of this story in scripture, but the amount of gossip that went on in the palace over this event must have been perpetually whispered about because the result in Michal's life was barrenness. There seems to be a precedent set in her lifetime from the day of that event. She was stuck in a hurt. Now that would be the subject of a gossip mill. 2 Sam. 6:23 **Therefore Michal the daughter of Saul had no child unto the day of her death.**

Michal could have repented of her anger and malicious thoughts toward David because there was grace in the covenant for that. Yet, she was bound by the words that came out in the heated argument until her death. Had the continual gossip taken on a life of its own, thus keeping Michal bound by her own anger? Was the hurt a tool of the enemy to keep Michal justifying her anger and thus creating a self-barrenness? I'm not sure, but it is a sad story like so many other sad stories that never get resolved because of anger and the gossip that keeps it going.

Words give life or death. The way we use them can bring healing or destruction. We have been given the power of words by our Creator to create an Eden or a Hell for ourselves and everyone we meet. Psalm 19:14 **Let the words of my mouth, and the meditation of my heart, be acceptable in thy sight, O LORD, my strength, and my redeemer.** May it be said of us who follow Christ that we took our tongues and did not lend them to gossip, but used them to bring about the blessing of the Kingdom of God.

Our tongues were bought along with the rest of us at the Cross of the Lord Jesus. As my friend Jami Rogers says, "I'm not for sale. I have already been bought and paid for in full by the Lord Jesus." Our lives and everything about our lives belong to the Lord, and that includes our words that proceed out of our mouths.

Interesting that the Proverb indicates that anger is one of the results of gossip. Prov. 25:23 **As surely as a north wind brings rain, so a gossiping tongue causes anger!** If we were to cut down on gossip, would that cut down on the anger that is in this world? The only way we are going to find out is to stop the fine art of gossiping that has wormed its way into our everyday conversations. Prov. 18:21 **Death and life are in the power of the tongue: and they that love it shall eat the fruit thereof.** May the Lord help us all overcome this sin. Amen!

GO MAKE DISCIPLES

Proverbs 22:20 Have not I written to thee excellent things in counsels and knowledge?

One of the last instructions that was given to the followers of Christ by the Lord Jesus before He was taken up into glory was that we, His followers, were to go and make disciples of all nations.

The reason we could do this work with all confidence and assurance was that all power in heaven and earth has been given to Jesus, who has given it to us for the task of bringing the Kingdom of God to all nations. Matt. 28:18 **And Jesus came and spake unto them, saying, All power is given unto me in heaven and in earth. 19 Therefore, go and make disciples of all the nations, baptizing them in the name of the Father and the Son and the Holy Spirit.**

Along with this instruction was we are to disciple the nations. Matt. 28:20 **Teaching them to observe all things whatsoever I have commanded you: and, lo, I am with you alway, even unto the end of the world. Amen.** There it is, the discipleship mandate: "Teaching them to observe all things whatsoever I have commanded you."

Anyone who has walked with the Lord for any significant amount of time can disciple any new Christian. If we have been walking in the obedience of the Lord, then we have a lifetime of lessons we can teach the next generation who are desperate for mentors and guidance in the word of God. Yet so many of the older Christians are waiting for some kind of burning-bush experience to set them on their way to become a hand extended to help make disciples.

Why they are waiting is a mystery, because the word of God has already said to go and do it. The Lord would not have told everyone to go and make disciples if it were not possible. I have asked some of the Christians who have walked for years in their faith why they were not taking up the mandate of discipling someone. Their lame and pathetic answer is normally "I do not know enough yet."

God is not asking you to teach them a theological thesis on the ark of the covenant and its many facets. He just wants you to help, guide, and pray with the people who are starting out their walk in Christ. He wants you to be an armor bearer for the new saints who are testing their new spiritual weapons they will have to work with throughout their lives. Eph. 6:11 **Put on the whole armour of God, that ye may be able to stand against the wiles of the devil.** All new Christians need help getting fitted with their new spiritual clothing. You can help them adjust so they can become victorious in Christ.

In the Gospel of Mark, chapter five, we read the story of the demoniac of Gadara. This man was possessed by a legion of demons. He was in absolute torment. Mark 5:5 **And always, night and day, he was in the**

mountains, and in the tombs, crying, and cutting himself with stones. He could not be controlled with shackles or irons because he would break them.

His life was a total hell all day long. He spots Jesus and comes running to Him. The Lord delivers him from the evil spirit. Mark 5:8 **For he said unto him, Come out of the man, thou unclean spirit. 9 And he asked him, What is thy name? And he answered, saying, My name is Legion: for we are many.** After this miraculous deliverance, the man is in his right mind and clothed for the first time in a long time.

At this point, the man who had been possessed wants to follow Jesus, but Jesus says something amazing. Mark 5:19 **Howbeit Jesus suffered him not, but saith unto him, Go home to thy friends, and tell them how great things the Lord hath done for thee, and hath had compassion on thee. 20 And he departed, and began to publish in Decapolis how great things Jesus had done for him: and all men did marvel.**

What? No instruction to go to bible college, countless amount of seminars, or years sitting in church? Jesus said, "Go tell your friends what the Lord has done for you in compassion." Go disciple with what you have and more will be given to you.

We are a generation who have so much biblical information that many of us have forgotten more than the next generation will ever learn. That is an indictment against what Christ has freely done in our lives. Luke 12:48b **From everyone who has been given much, much will be demanded; and from the one who has been entrusted with much, much more will be asked.**

I have been most fortunate throughout the years to always have someone I am mentoring in Christ. Young and old, I have been blessed to go and make disciples by showing them what the Lord has done for me and within my life. I meet with different people and in different languages for a few hours a week to help answer questions that new believers come up with. The interesting thing is the fruit and reward in my life have been magnificent.

God is always faithful to give the information needed in all situations. We just have to be willing to be a servant of the Lord. We need to jerk the slack out of our excuses and disobedience. Most of us can disciple. We just have to want to do it. Phil. 4:13 **I can do all things through Christ which strengthens me.** May God give us the strength to step forward and be counted. God Bless you richly.

BENEDICTION

Heavenly Father, please bless all the readers who have taken the time to read this book. May the Lord's face shine on each one of them and give them the desires of their hearts.

Through lessons gleaned from each chapter, enable them to overcome all the attacks of the enemy. Remind them in the midst of their battles that Christ has made us overcomers in this life.

May recall knowledge of the scriptures they read fill them with peace.

May God direct them to accomplish all God has for them, and may everyone be fulfiled. In Jesus name!

INDEX TO FEATURED PROVERBS

About The Authour

When I first accepted Christ as my Lord in the late 1970s, I had a hard time reading and writing. However, the blessing I did have in my life at that time was that God had given me the ability to remember scripture when I heard it and read it slowly.

I have been in Christian ministry in one form or another for about forty years. I attended Commonwealth Bible College in Katoomba, New South Wales, Australia, in 1980. Ministry at that time involved prison ministries, preaching on the radio in a small town, and church-related works of all kinds. I have taught bible college courses and also have been involved in personal discipleship training. God has blessed me all along the way. Now I have the opportunity to write down what was experienced throughout the years.

As someone who was once functionally illiterate, I can appreciate the work it takes to get a book written and published. The Lord has blessed me with sound, strong, and forthright material to write a series of Christian devotionals. I have lived the testimonies on these pages and can attest to the fact that God is so faithful and good. My hope is that your soul will be enriched as you read this book. God bless you and give you the desires of your heart.

CONNECT WITH NORM

Norm's Blog "Sir Norm's Proverbial Comment" can be found online in English, French and Spanish. Your comments on any of the hundreds of blog posts are appreciated.

Sir Norm's Proverbial Comment:
https://sirnorm1.blogspot.ca/

Commentaire Proverbial de Sir Norm:
https://sirnorm.blogspot.ca/

Comentario Proverbial de Sir Norm:
https://sirnorm-1.blogspot.ca/

First Page Solutions Author Page:
https://firstpagesolutions.ca/publisher/author/norm-sawyer/